THE

CEDARTOWN

HIGH SCHOOL

BULLDOGS

THE
CEDARTOWN
HIGH SCHOOL
BULLDOGS

THE HISTORY OF A GEORGIA FOOTBALL TRADITION

WILLIAM AUSTIN

Charleston · London

THE
History
PRESS

Published by The History Press
Charleston, SC 29403
www.historypress.net

Copyright © 2012 by William Austin
All rights reserved

First published 2012

Manufactured in the United States

ISBN 978.1.60949.706.4

Library of Congress CIP data applied for.

CONTENTS

ACKNOWLEDGEMENTS

This book was written primarily from newspaper articles from the *Cedartown Standard* and the *Rome News Tribune*. Heather Gray researched the articles. She spent many hours looking through the microfilm at the Cedartown Library. Other sources include: the Polk County Historical Society (provided most of the photographs), Keilas Photo Lab (reproducing photos), Georgia High School Historians Association (a valuable source for game scores, region alignments, ranking polls, all-state players and other information), the Georgia Archives (photos), Doc Ayers (photos), Dr. Jerry Weaver (scrapbook), Lloyd Gray Jr. (yearbooks), Greg Roberson (photos and articles), Frank Lott Jr. (photos), Greg Gray (photos and newspaper articles), Frank Burgess Jr. (interview), Don Smith (photos and articles), Mrs. Dave Roberson (photos), Gail Conner (photos), Wikipedia (verifying sources), *Athens Banner* (archives) and Milt Shaw (technical support). Most of all, thank you to my wife, Jeanene, for her support and patience while I spent hundreds of hours researching and writing this book about my favorite team.

INTRODUCTION

G oing into halftime with a two-touchdown lead, all the Cedartown football team needed to do was win two quarters of football and they would make history. Twenty-four minutes of football and the 2001 Bulldogs would be the first Cedartown High School team to win a state championship on their home field in the ninety-eight years they had been playing football. They have one official state championship to their credit and other unofficial championships that have been lost with the crumbling of newspapers and scrapbooks or forgotten by aging memories. There were hard times following the 1963 state championship team that has engraved itself into immortality. Doc Ayers had set up a system that ran two and three squads deep. He left his hallmark as a leader who turned a bunch of country boys into football players. When Vince Dooley took over as head coach for the University of Georgia, Doc Ayers was the first assistant coach he hired. Several enthusiastic assistant coaches with high hopes wanted to take the helm of the Bulldogs. Ray Carter got the nod over some coaches who went on to have successful careers at other schools. Coach Carter was the first to realize that what Doc Ayers could do wasn't a mere walk in the park, especially in those times.

Three more coaches would follow Ray Carter before the team returned to prominence. They were all good men and were probably better coaches than their records reflect. With social issues like President Kennedy's assassination, the Vietnam War, integration and a mood to shun competition sweeping across the nation, they all found that following a coaching legend proved to be an insurmountable task.

Finally, in 1976, the community and, more importantly, the boys in the community were ready to bring the Bulldogs back to the forefront and reestablish Cedartown as a football town. The fact of the matter is that it is the youngsters in the town who make up the football team. If the top athletes do not try out for the team, it is impossible to compete with other schools that have their best players suited up to play every week. Every community has enough high school age boys who, if given the right training and equipment, are capable of winning a state championship.

This book is dedicated to Frank "Red" Lott, left end of the undefeated 1928 team. Forever a Bulldog, Red lost his life when he was shot by an unknown gunman while answering a burglary alarm at Cedartown High School. *Courtesy of Frank Lott Jr.*

When Coach John Hill arrived, he brought with him a kid who had a rifle arm and a total understanding of his offensive scheme. It didn't take the eager lads from Cedartown long to catch on to the system and catch on to winning, as they won ten games the first year. Quarterback Ted Peeples renewed the tradition of great Cedartown quarterbacks. Over the next twenty-five years, several Cedartown quarterbacks would earn scholarships and play football for Division I colleges. The number of players who went on to play other positions at all levels of college competition is staggering. When John Hill came to town, he introduced northwest Georgia to a new brand of football. With his motto, "Respect all, but fear none," he transformed a team that had been in a fifteen-year drought into a state powerhouse.

This team in 2001 was the team of reckoning that he had been trying to build for twenty-five years. Hill and his 'Dogs had been close on several occasions. He had teams that ran the table and were undefeated in the regular seasons but fell in the playoffs against tough teams like Dalton and Marist. In 1985, a ragtag group of hard hitters rebounded from early season losses and went on a run that didn't end until they hit a brick wall in the state championship game in Thomson. There were several advances into the

10

quarterfinals and a couple of visits to the semifinals in the Georgia Dome that served notice that CHS was here to stay.

Superstars like Jeff Burger, Brian Burgdorf and Ken Veal had come through the Cedartown system and went on to have successful college careers at Auburn, Alabama and Georgia, but no Cedartown team was as skilled in every position as this 2001 team. There were no weak links on this team. From shoulder to shoulder and backfield to backfield, the team lined up quality athletes at every position and carried out its assignments with precision and tenacity. Now, with all the pieces in place, Coach Hill retired, and the program was handed over to longtime assistant Everett Kelley.

Kelley had been on Hill's staff for many years and served as assistant head coach in waiting. He took the task to hand and put the final touches on the strong foundation that Coach Hill had left behind. The team improved each game as they rolled over top teams and were undefeated going into the championship game. From the look of things, they had saved the best for last, as they had the Grangers against the ropes and were looking to deliver the knockout blow.

In the first half, Cedartown's Matt Robinson picked up a fumble and was running for a touchdown when he was caught from behind and had the ball stripped out of his hands by LaGrange quarterback Blake Mitchell. That play could have opened the floodgates, as the Cedartown defense had kept the Granger offense under control.

The Cedartown defense stymied the LaGrange offense that was rated one of the best in Georgia. On offense, Drew Robinson slashed through the line for six and seven yards each carry, while Kendrick Sewell hit them for big gainers on the corners.

There was a fantastic feeling of pride as the team ran onto the field for the second half in their traditional uniforms of silver pants, red jerseys and silver helmets with no stripes, emblems or decorations other than the white numbers and the letter "C" on both sleeves. They had worn the same uniforms for years, and even though they looked very simple, those uniforms represented power and class. Inside every uniform was a teenage boy who was confident, well prepared and truly believed that he and his teammates were going to win the game.

What happened in the third and fourth quarters is a continuing debate. Some people believe that the Cedartown coaching staff became complacent, and instead of unleashing their powerful offense, they called safe, ineffective plays and relied on their great defense to hold the line and win the game. Others say that losing star running back Kendrick Sewell to injury allowed

LaGrange to key on fullback Drew Robinson and shut down the running game. Others simply believe that the best team won.

Quarterback Mitchell discovered the holes in the Cedartown secondary and connected with his receivers. With less than a minute to play, he lobbed a pass just out of reach of the Cedartown defender and completed the winning touchdown pass that crushed the hearts of the team and its fans.

Many of these players returned to play in 2002 but stumbled at the start. They lost the second game of the season to a Towers High team that everyone believes they should have beaten. A few weeks later, they lost a rematch with LaGrange by ten points. Once again, these veteran players shook off the loss and rolled on through the regular season. They won two playoff games but were defeated in the quarterfinals on the road in Dublin, Georgia. There was a crucial momentum swing when a questionable celebration or taunting penalty was called on Drew Robinson after he sacked the elusive Dublin quarterback. What would have been a ten-yard loss, giving Dublin a fourth down around the fifty-yard line, suddenly became a first down around the ten-yard line. Dublin punched the ball into the end zone, which gave them the go-ahead score and all the momentum as the clock began to tick away.

The year 2003 was the first noticeable slip, as Cedartown won the first six games but ended the season on a four-game losing streak and didn't make the playoffs for the first time in five years.

When the team slipped to four wins and six losses in 2004, a big rumbling commenced that led to the resignation of Coach Kelley. Throughout Hill's reign, there had been some down times, some break-even seasons and even losing seasons. It was unfortunate that Coach Kelley wasn't able to put his career at CHS against the test of time and find out if he could have revived the program. Now living and coaching in Alabama, Everett makes his daily drive to work along the Georgia state line. With Cedartown being a stone's throw away, there isn't a day that goes by that Everett doesn't look to the east and wonder—what could have been?

Young Matt Hollis, a Washington County and Rick Tomberlain protégé, was brought in from Forsyth Central to lead the team. In his three years as a head coach at Forsyth, Hollis had a combined record of five wins and twenty-five losses. Someone obviously saw something that led him to believe that Hollis was the coach that would put Cedartown football on the right track. It was a disaster. There should be an offer of empathy for the young coach who got in way over his head in a town that expected to win with a wide-open offense and a quarterback who could throw the ball twenty or thirty times a game. Had Matt Hollis done his homework and hired an effective offensive coordinator, he might still be the head coach of the Cedartown Bulldogs, because his defense was one of the best in the state. Instead, it was three wins and a quick exit for Hollis, as things got worse for the Bulldogs.

Mark Loudermilk had success as the head coach at Trion but had losing seasons the two years prior to his move to Cedartown. The downward trend continued when he reached Cedar Valley; he went winless in his debut season. Finally, the mighty dog had fallen into the depths of despair. Try as he would, Mr. Loudermilk could only achieve one break-even season and one trip to the playoffs.

During Loudermilk's tenure, the dreaded cycle set in. The team wasn't winning, and no one wanted to play for a losing team that had no fans in the bleachers. There were no more incentives like college scholarships. When Sam Hunt finished his playing career with the University of Alabama at Birmingham, it was the first time in years that there were no Cedartown role models playing football in the college games on Saturday.

Organized football is a tough and demanding game. As a matter of fact, most of the time players spend putting their bodies through grueling training exercises and conditioning drills has nothing to do with a football and certainly can't be defined as playing. As the cycle continues, fewer players produce a less competitive team for which no one wants to play.

In 2010, Scott Hendrix became the head coach of the Cedartown Bulldogs. In two seasons, he has been able to bring the Bulldogs back to a competitive level. Junior quarterback Zack Chubb used quick feet, smart decisions and open field speed to keep Cedartown in every game. He caught the attention of many college recruiters and was offered a coveted scholarship to play football for the U.S. Air Force Academy in Colorado.

In 2011, his younger brother, Nick Chubb, joined him in the backfield to give Cedartown one of the most explosive running attacks in the state. The young sophomore gained over 1,500 yards running the football. After nearly pulling off the region championship, the 'Dogs held a 7–6 lead over Stephens County. A late Indian touchdown ended an exciting season for the Bulldogs.

There is a wealth of talent coming from the middle school and the junior varsity. Coach Hendrix and his staff seem to have the right formula to get the most from his players as Cedartown could be on an upward trend.

CHAPTER 1

A NEW TOWN IS BORN

Cedar Town was the name the Creek Indians gave to a trading post in northwest Georgia that sat next to a cold natural spring in the heart of a fertile valley that was covered with red cedar trees. The Creeks claimed possession of the land and were constantly fighting with the Cherokee Indians for control of the region. The story is that one day they decided to end the feud and settle the ownership of the land by playing a ballgame. The popular story is that the ballgame was somewhat similar to the game of baseball, but knowing the hearts and minds of the people who have come out of Cedar Valley, it is more likely that the game was more like football. Whichever game they played, the Cherokees were the victors and the Creeks were sent packing for lands farther to the south. The spring was a peaceful place for Indians and white pioneers to gather and trade their goods and learn about one another's way of life.

The first white settlers arrived in the Cedartown area in 1826, when Linton Walthall and Hampton Whatley visited the area amidst the backdrop of the beautiful Indian Mountains. They returned in 1830, built stores and established the first white community in the area, calling it Big Springs. In 1832, despite a Supreme Court ruling that prevented the takeover of Indian lands, President Andrew Jackson allowed the deeding and purchasing of all the land in Georgia that was occupied by Indians. Asa Prior moved into the area and purchased huge blocks of land that stretched from Big Springs to the Alabama state line.

Cedartown High School on College Street opened in 1898. *Courtesy of Polk County Historical Society.*

The 1903 Cedartown Bulldogs. *First row, left to right*: Charles Rob Borders, Dean Daws (mascot), Lewis Wood; *second row*: Will E. Roberts, T.O. Marshall, Charles James, Ed Fraizer, Walt Bunn, Gus Henderson; *third row*: Malcolm Bradford, Tom Judkins, Cliff Hightower. *Courtesy of Polk County Historical Society.*

Mystery photo believed to have been taken around 1914. *Courtesy of Polk County Historical Society.*

Prior donated twenty acres of land to the newly formed Polk County. In 1852, a courthouse was built and the town of Cedartown was created.

Cedartown survived the brunt of the Civil War until near the end of the war, when General Kilpatrick's cavalry burned the courthouse and most of the town. The town struggled to survive as the state withdrew its charter. The citizens, still too devastated from the destruction of the war, all but gave up on Cedartown. Finally, the people became revitalized, and in 1867, a new courthouse was built.

Soon the farms began to reappear and the community began to heal. In 1873, ironmaster Amos West from Connecticut built the Cherokee Iron Works to take advantage of the huge iron ore deposits in Polk County. He built a blast furnace that at its peak produced fifty tons of pig iron per day.

In 1878, William Noyes established the first Cedartown High School. Students were required to pay tuition fees for the wide variety of classes that were offered. The community began to prosper in 1896, when Charles

The 1916 Cedartown Bulldogs. *First row, left to right*: Glenn Underwood, George Collins, Jack Williams, Carlton Purks, Hall Hackney, C.J. Turner; *second row*: Horace Edmondson, Victor Camarata, Robert Spinks, Lewis Pitts; *third row*: Tony Camarata, Charlie "Monk" Pittman, Brooks McMorrow, Edwin Jones, Wink Philpot, Raymong Parris, Clyde Bobo, Boyd Garner. *Courtesy of Polk County Historical Society.*

Adamson built the Cedartown Cotton Manufacturing Company and bought out other cotton mills in the area.

In 1900, Cedartown had a population of 2,823, L.S. Ledbetter was the mayor and it was illegal to pass the football forward or beyond the line of scrimmage. The forward pass was made legal in 1906. By now, football was becoming a popular sport for high school boys. Charles Brumby said that Cedartown played Rockmart in a game of football on November 22, 1900. The *Atlanta Constitution* reported that a game between Cedartown and Rome was scheduled for Thanksgiving 1902.

CHAPTER 2

A TRADITION IS BUILT

1916–1918

The 1916 team was one of Cedartown's first competitive teams. Under the direction of Professor H.L. Sewell, players Tony Camarata and Clyde Bobo took over the daily coaching duties called the plays and set the defensive alignments. The team had strength and agility to go along with a fierceness and desire to win. The offensive power came from quarterback Jack Williams and halfbacks C.J. Turner and Lewis Pitts. Wink Philpot provided the tough inside running at fullback.

The Bulldogs began the season with a 13–7 loss to Rome. The *Rome News* described the scrappy Cedartown team as being "endowed with pugilistic tendencies."

The next week, the 'Dogs went on the road and hammered cross-county rival Rockmart (61–0) on Wednesday and brought down the axe on Marietta (26–0) on Friday. Once again, the strong running and powerful tackling of Pitts, Philpot and Turner led the way for the boys from Cedartown.

Things got a bit tougher for Cedartown when Cartersville's Purple Hurricane blew onto the West Avenue field. Cedartown's offense continually moved the ball deep inside Cartersville territory but was only able to break into the end zone one time to pull even for a 6–6 tie.

There was an interesting write-up in the *Cedartown Standard* about a game between Cedartown and Newnan. The article is about Newnan's coach, Charles Brown, who doubled as the umpire for the game. There were people of notoriety who were listed in the article who claimed that Brown made several questionable calls that helped Newnan go ahead 14–0. In the second half, when Cedartown was driving the ball at will on Newnan and about to tie the game, Brown forfeited the game because Cedartown was "rough housing" the Newnan players.

In 1918, T.M. Smith took over as head coach. Now that the players were becoming notorious, they began taking on nicknames such as Neighbor Hackney, Tomcat Lemon, Shorty Spinks, Peewee Griffin, Horsecollar Williams, Blubber Pitts and Foxy Philpot. The young celebrities found out early in the season that no opponent was going to lie down for them when they made the trip to Cartersville and fought for their lives to preserve a 6–6 tie.

Against Marietta, the 'Dogs had several impressive drives and looked like the better football team, but Marietta completed some long passes that kept them in the game and managed a 13–13 tie.

1919

The first team to visit Cedartown in 1919 was the Rome Hilltoppers. An eighty-yard run by Carlton Purks was the highlight of the game. Tony Camarata caught two touchdowns passes, and C.J. Turner scored three times as the Bulldogs started the season with a win.

Next was a game that went beyond the boundaries of good sportsmanship and fair play when Cedartown traveled to Marietta. An article in the *Cedartown Standard*, written by Coach T.M. Smith, tells the story of how Marietta used a combination of Marietta schoolboys, Marietta town men, and four players from the Georgia Tech second team. Coach Smith writes in his article that he went to the Marietta principal and told him that Cedartown's team was composed of bona fide high school players who were expecting to play bona fide students. The principal gave Smith his assurance that only high school students would be playing. During the game, there was a rumbling in the crowd that Marietta had planned to use some ringers from Georgia Tech. One Georgia Tech student who was from Cedartown identified one player as McClesky, who played end and had lettered for Georgia Tech. Smith went to the principal and demanded that McClesky be taken out of the game, but the principal refused. Smith then went on to pull the Cedartown team off the field, and the referees told him that if he wouldn't forfeit the game, they would remove McClesky and the other three Tech lettermen. Marietta had a two-touchdown lead, and with the loss of C.J Turner due to injuries, the Bulldogs were not able to come back and suffered their first defeat of the season.

The next week the Bulldogs ventured across the state line to play Gadsden, Alabama. The Alabama boys went right to work and drove the ball down the field to take a 6–0 lead in the first quarter. The CHS defense stiffened as both teams' defenses dominated the first half.

Cedartown received the ball to open the second half and drove the ball inside Gadsden's twenty-yard line but gave up the ball on downs. Gadsden ran three plays and punted to C.J. Turner, who eluded two defenders as he turned the corner and raced for the score. In the fourth quarter, Tony Camarata caught a short pass and outran the defense for a forty-five-yard touchdown. The final score was 13–6, but when the clock ran out, Cedartown was driving the ball for another score. Hall Hackney and C.J. Turner were beginning to shred the Gadsden line for fifteen- and twenty-yard gains. The team and the fans received "royal treatment" from the Gadsden community. This was due to the efforts of Miss Opal Hall, who was once a student at Cedartown High School.

Returning home, the 'Dogs set their sights on the college prep team from Marist, one of the fastest teams in the state. Coach Smith was confident that his boys would be up to the task of keeping pace with the boys from Atlanta. The game was hotly contested from start to finish, but the Cedartown boys prevailed 6–0.

Coming up on Thanksgiving Day was the rematch with Marietta on Cedartown's home field. After using players from Georgia Tech to give the 'Dogs their only loss of the season, everybody was anxious to see just who Marietta would bring along for the contest. Without sending a notice or explanation, Marietta's football team never arrived to play Cedartown on Thanksgiving Day. With a final record of six wins and one defeat, Cedartown was crowned District 7 champion.

CHAPTER 3

THE 1920s

1920

In 1920, the population of Cedartown was 4,853. H.M. Hall was the mayor, and iron ore and textile production peaked in West Polk County. The 1920s would see the largest growth in the town's history, as Cedartown grew to 8,123 residents by 1930, making it the nineteenth-largest city in Georgia.

On October 15, the CHS Bulldogs gave a rude welcome to visiting Griffin High at the West Avenue Athletic Park with a score of 28–0.

Disque High School from Gadsden, Alabama, rolled in to Cedartown to take on the 'Dogs but limped away the loser after a brutal defensive battle. Camarata picked up a fumble and tossed it to John Good, who ran it in for the only score of the game, as both defenses dominated the game. Gadsden drove down to Cedartown's three-yard line, but the 'Dogs held them until the half ran out. Late in the game, the Bulldogs drove to the Gadsden one-yard line but were unable to punch the ball in for the score. The 7–0 victory was a sweet win for Cedartown.

The 'Dogs took to the road and traveled to Athens, Georgia, where they were handily defeated 27–7. The *Athens Banner* noted that Cedartown was considered to be the west Georgia champion and Athens High was considered the east Georgia champion.

The next week, the Rome Hilltoppers were scheduled to visit Cedartown, but because of a barrage of injuries to the players, the Romans were forced to cancel. Wanting to play football, Cedartown contracted to play the Alabama

Normal School from Jacksonville, Alabama. A normal school was a school for high school graduates to be trained as teachers. Since there was no age limits for college-level players, the Bulldogs found themselves up against a team of tough men from Alabama who outweighed them on an average of thirty pounds. Gritting it out and playing some of their best football, the 'Dogs fought valiantly but were overwhelmed in the end and lost 14–0. The Alabama coach said that the Cedartown team was the hardest-hitting high school team he had ever seen. He said that the execution of plays and ball handling skills were excellent. The *Cedartown Standard* of December 9, 1920, reported, "Light weight, yes, but, O how they can play football! Have you seen them in action? Do you realize they are one of the top notchers in the whole state? Our team is something to be proud of."

In the last game of the season, Cedartown traveled to Gadsden with a rematch with Disque, where the score was turned around to be 7–0 in favor of the home team. Cedartown dominated the game but could not score. The Disque touchdown came on a controversial play that involved an illegal forward pass.

The Cedartown merchants awarded sweaters to the players of the team. The sweaters were black with the letter "C" in red. Receiving sweaters were John Camarata, Glenn York, Wesley Hanley, Marion Roberts, John Good, Clarence Nation, Clyde Suggs, Liddell Griffith, Charles Sewell, Alton Judkins, Cecil Cornelius, Clifton Harris, Clarence Barrett, George Mundy, George Simerville and Edouard Benton. At the presentation, head coach Professor T.M Smith praised the team for having a great season especially when going against teams that were much bigger.

1921

On September 30, 1921, a new library opened on College Street. Mr. A.K. Hawkes, a philanthropist from Atlanta, donated $7,500 for its construction. Local residents added another $15,000 in order that the building might be a city ornament. The handsome building still stands today and is the home of the Polk County Historical Museum.

After bombarding Cartersville with 62 points, the 1921 Bulldogs, coached by Professor W.L. Monts, were unable to find that scoring punch against Carrollton. The Trojans' hefty line of scrimmage outweighed, outmuscled and outfought the 'Dogs as they tagged Cedartown with a 6–0 loss.

After getting trounced 27–7 by Marietta, the team found itself in a downward trend when it encountered a newly energized Cartersville team. In a freewheeling game filled with forearms and elbows, it was all the 'Dogs could do to salvage a 7–7 tie.

Marietta came to Cedartown the next week and pulled another one of its tricks of playing ringers from Georgia Tech. After a battle that ended in a 6–6 tie, the *Cedartown Standard* complimented both teams for their tough aggressive play but chastised Marietta about sportsmanship and fair play. The writer for the newspaper suggested that if they were "encouraging dishonest practices, the boys had better take their exercise on the rock-pile."

Following losses to Carrollton and Disque High of Gadsden, the Bulldogs closed out a less than stellar season with a 6–0 win over Marietta.

1922

Professor Reynolds took over as coach of the Bulldogs in 1922. Commercial High of Atlanta came to Cedartown to kick off the 1922 season and found the going too tough as the 'Dogs exploded for a 56–0 victory. The new uniforms were well reflected by the play of what some people believed was the best football team Cedartown had ever put on the field.

A 50–0 shattering of Chickamauga set up a showdown with top-ranked Carrollton. Although they were outweighed, the Bulldogs proved that they had the metal to pound on the Carrollton line until they came away with a 9–0 victory.

Cedartown continued to roll with a 50–0 win over Rhinehart College and a 36–0 win over the Fourth District A&M. Coach Camarata cited the speed of Hunt and Edmondson at the halfback positions, along with the punt returns by Mundy, as key offensive contributors. He lauded the play of offensive linemen Suggs, Judkins and John Rusk. On the defensive side of the ball, he pointed out the aggressive plays of Edwin Janes and Jack McElveen, who broke up several trick plays. He also praised the good tackling by Barrett.

All of North Georgia was anticipating the matchup between Cedartown and the University of Atlanta Prep School. The city was dressed in full attire as a parade marched down Main Street to celebrate the great event. The stores closed from 2:30 to 4:30 p.m. on the day of the big game as thousands filled the bleachers and lined the field to watch a hard-hitting football game.

The boys from Atlanta were bigger, faster and older than the Cedartown boys. In the end, it was the physical maturity that made the difference in the game. The 'Dogs fought hard and kept it close until the final minutes, when the University of Atlanta put up two scores and won 27–0. Although they went down in defeat, the Bulldogs gained statewide notoriety, as the *Atlanta Journal* covered the game. The ticket sales from the huge crowd would go a long way in helping the team meet its expenses.

The next week, the 'Dogs returned to their winning ways with a 14–0 win over Cartersville.

The 1922 Cedartown Bulldogs were not scored on by any high school team and were only defeated by Presbyterian College and the University of Atlanta. They were considered to be the North Georgia champions and one of the best football teams of the state.

1923

Professor Reynolds would have a tough task of rebuilding his team after the previous undefeated season. Practically every player on the team was in his first year of competition for the Bulldogs. Bill Mundy and Clifford Harris returned to anchor the line, but linemen Oliver Wilson, Hoke Hamrick, Ross Timms, Hampton Hackney and Cecil Carter would be making their first starts. The backfield of quarterback Cleveland Barrett, halfbacks Bill Tyler and Willard Walker and fullback J.B. Brown had a cumulative total of zero playing minutes. Marvin Waters, Buddy Young, Max Chapman and Francis Simerville rounded out the 1923 Cedartown Bulldogs.

The first order of business for the young pups was to go over to Rockmart and claim the title of Polk County champions. Barrett and Chapman led the way for the Cedartown win.

Once again, it was Barrett along with Carter who made strong offensive showings against the Fourth District A&M from Carrollton as the 'Dogs took a 13–6 win. Harris and Hamrick were noted for their line play.

In the next game, Barrett scored one touchdown early in the game and another late in the game to give Cedartown a 14–9 win over Cartersville.

On Thanksgiving Day, the boys in black waded through buckets of mud to scavenge a 13–13 tie with Hearn Institute from Cave Spring. Once again, it was Barrett who scored both touchdowns for Cedartown. Earlier losses to Rome and Marietta were the only blemishes on the 1923 Bulldogs' record.

1924

The Bulldogs got off on the wrong foot in 1924 by losing to the prep school Carrollton A&M, formerly known as the Fourth District A&M, by a score of 26–0. Cedartown was outmatched as the bigger and older young men controlled the line of scrimmage and moved the ball at will. It wasn't exactly what new coach Shuler Antley had hoped for in his debut at Cedartown.

The work of Carl Carter and Bill Mundy was noted as the Bulldogs beat Piedmont High 14–0 in Alabama.

Carter and Young played well against Rockmart, giving Cedartown a 6–0 win.

One of the state's top teams from LaFayette brought in a large crowd of supporters only to be sent home the disappointed loser to a Bulldog team that was beginning to take the championship form that was expected of Cedartown teams. It was a nail-biting defensive struggle that kept the crowd on the edge of its seats as the 'Dogs won another tight contest 6–0.

The 1924 Cedartown Bulldogs. *First row, left to right*: W.W. Mundy Jr., Donald Busby, Russell Brown, William Biggers, A.E. Young (captain), Homer Edwards, Spencer Smith, Max Chapman, Carl Spencer; *second row*: Harry Nuttall, C.R. Brumby Jr., Sam Coffee, Roy Underwood, Francis Simerville, Paul Stevens, G.H. Edwards, R. Timms, William Tyler, Coach Schuler Antley. *Courtesy of Polk County Historical Society*.

1925

Dalton was first on the Cedartown agenda for 1925, and the 'Dogs were true to form, whipping the Catamounts 19–0. The game was knotted at zero at halftime, but Charles Brumby broke through in the second half for two scores, and Whitlow Wyatt scored once. The winning streak reached four games when the 'Dogs mauled the Carrollton Trojans 45–13.

Buddy Young, Whitlow Wyatt, Charles Brumby and Russell Brown were called the "Four Horsemen," as they galloped around their opponents and ran roughshod over the defensive line. The Four Horsemen had one of their best games when they defeated a bigger and heavier LaFayette team 10–0. Brown scored all of Cedartown's points. He scored the touchdown, kicked the extra point and made the field goal.

November 12, 1925, marked the first issue of the Cedartown High School newspaper, the *Red and Black*. The paper was carried along with the *Cedartown Standard* and was written by CHS students. The first headline read, "Cedartown Defeats Marietta 6–0! Chickamauga Here Tomorrow."

Marietta was a tough win. Early in the first quarter, Cedartown fumbled inside Marietta's one-yard line. From that point on, most of the game was played in Cedartown's territory, but time and again the Bulldogs hunkered down and kept Marietta out of the end zone. Late in the fourth quarter, an interference call set up Homer Edwards's run for the only score of the game.

Chickamauga used a combination of fancy footwork and slick ball handling to keep the Bulldogs at bay for the first few minutes of the game. In the second quarter, Cedartown put together a drive that culminated with Tom Hunt going in for the score. In the second half, Edwards, Bunn Wood, Brown and Hunt made several long Red Grange–type runs that ended on a Hunt scoring run.

Cedartown made it nine in a row without a loss by trouncing Tallapoosa 28–0.

There were too many stars to name as Coach Antley's Bulldogs beat Cartersville to win their tenth game with no losses. The year 1925 was a perfect season for a great team. LaGrange, Gainesville and Americus were the only other teams in the state of Georgia to have undefeated seasons.

At the team banquet, held at the Wayside Inn, player Bill Tyler spoke to all the guests about how the team met for prayer before each game. He said that they didn't ask for victory. He said they asked "that they might play the game straight and meet and part with their opponents as friends."

1926

The year 1926 was one for rebuilding and breaking in a new coach. Professor Antley stepped aside and made way for Professor Bella Lancaster. In the first game against Cave Spring, the coach wasn't very happy with the play and production of his offense, so he held practice until it was nearly dark to get the team prepared for games against Carrollton and LaFayette. The team found its stride just in time, as it looked like teams of old when it took down the Ramblers by a score of 32–0. Whitlow Wyatt, Sam Coffee, Roy Underwood and Frank Lott were noted for outstanding play.

The 'Dogs ran into a roadblock when they took on the Atlanta University School for Boys. The Bluebirds were bigger, heavier and simply outclassed Cedartown. Wyatt scored the only touchdown for Cedartown.

Cedartown traveled south to take on a powerful LaGrange team that was riding a long winning streak. Although the 'Dogs were trying to rebound

The 1926 Cedartown Bulldogs. Red Lott is standing next to Coach Bella Lancaster. Bunn Wood is standing at the far right. Sitting second from left is Dippy Wyatt, and fourth from left is Ed Barrett. *Courtesy of Frank Lott Jr.*

after losing to the Atlanta preparatory school, the town of LaGrange was excited about Cedartown's visit. According to the October 28 *Cedartown Standard*, "LaGrange closed all her business houses and you couldn't even buy an ice cream cone Friday when our boys went there to play football." The enthusiasm rubbed off on the players, as the Grangers socked the Bulldogs 33–2.

The Bulldogs rebounded as Wyatt rambled for five touchdowns as Cedartown defeated Canton 45–0. Coach Lancaster had nothing but praise for his entire squad and especially the play of his defense.

Carrollton A&M sent over its band of "huskies" to go against the 'Dogs and ran into a smaller team that packed a powerful punch. When Wyatt wasn't splitting through the defensive line for long runs, he was spiraling the ball through the air for long pass completions. The big play was a sixty-yard touchdown pass to Howard West. Francis Simerville and Sam Coffee also had a big game. Six wins against three losses in a rebuilding year gave high marks to first-year coach Lancaster.

1927

In 1927, Coach Chambers joined the staff of Coach Lancaster at Cedartown. Lineman Roy Underwood was voted team captain.

The Bulldogs started the season on a good note by defeating LaFayette 36–6.

Injuries took their toll with the 1927 team and kept most of the Cedartown stars on the bench for most of the season. Big losses to Tech High in Atlanta and Canton High spoiled a season that saw the Bulldogs win five games and lose four. The 1927 players were: ends Frank Lott and Howard West; tackles Venable and Charles Brumby; guards "Punky" Pace and Hilburn; center Roy Underwood; quarterback Sam Coffee; fullback W. Wyatt; halfbacks Bunn Wood and Surls; and reserves Ed Barrett, Robert Wingard, Ayers, S. Edwards, B. Edwards, H. Wyatt and Hunt.

Whitlow Wyatt was offered a scholarship to play football for Georgia Tech, but the Detroit Tigers offered him $4,000 to play baseball. In 1941, Wyatt struck out Joe DiMaggio two times in the fifth game of the World Series. His ferocious inside fastball inspired DiMaggio to call him "the meanest man I ever saw." Off the field, Whitlow was a devoted family man who never crossed anyone. After a thirty-seven-year career of playing

and coaching in Major League Baseball, Whitlow retired to his farm in Haralson County, Georgia.

Bud Lott passed along a quip his father, "Red" Lott, made about Whitlow Wyatt: "If you were to get into a rock fight with Whitlow and managed to make it home, Whitlow could still hit you with a rock."

Whitlow Wyatt in his Brooklyn Dodgers uniform. *Courtesy of Polk County Historical Society.*

1928

Professor P.E. Parks announced that the 1928 school year would open with a record number of students enrolled at Cedartown schools.

"Jumping Jack" McElveen, who was a standout performer on the 1922 team, was killed in a skydiving accident in Florence, South Carolina. He was performing a daring parachute jump from about two thousand feet when a strap broke and caused him to hit the ground with great force. Jack had gained a lot of attention as a daring aviator for the Mabel Cody Air Circus.

Frank "Red" Lott was elected captain of the 1928 football team. Bunn Wood, one of the best running backs in CHS history, was elected alternate captain.

First up was an 88–0 pounding on Nelson High.

Then, Douglasville brought its eleven to town and went home a sore 20–0 loser.

There is another story that was passed down by Red Lott about a traveling salesman, Mr. Sconyers. Sconyers ran a sales route through Cedartown, Esom Hill and on into Alabama. It seems the man had an obsession with betting on football games. Late in the game, Cedartown was beating Carrollton 46–0. One of the players noticed that Sconyers seemed upset. When the player asked him why he was upset, the man told him that he had bet fifty dollars to a fellow in Alabama that Cedartown would beat Carrollton by more than fifty points. The player told Bunn Wood about it, and on Cedartown's next

The 1928 Cedartown Bulldogs. *First row, left to right*: Earl Dickerson, Bunn Wood, Ed Barrett, Harold Wyatt, Seals Edwards, John Howard, Lloyd Nichols, Roy Underwood, Robert Wingard, Orville Pace, Frank Lott; *second row*: Pat Simpson, Edgar Henderson, Buford Davis, Lofton Hunt, John Lankford, John Veal, Albert Stubbs, W.C. Cox, Glen Knighton, Jim White, Howard West; *third row*: Coach Lancaster, Howard Stewart, Glover Gray, Silas Nicholson, Joe Cleveland, Charles Edwards, Earl Swinney, Marshall Sutton, Milton Paris. *Courtesy of Frank Lott Jr.*

offensive series, Bunn made a thirty-yard touchdown run so that the man would win his bet.

A big crowd turned out in Chickamauga to see a hard-fought football game between two fine football teams. Bunn Wood scored the game's first touchdown on a short run around right end. In the third quarter, Chickamauga completed a pass to the Cedartown one-yard line. The Bulldogs stiffened their necks and held for three downs, but on fourth down, Chickamauga's running back ploughed through for the first points scored on Cedartown all year. With the clock winding down, Cedartown took over the ball on the fifty-yard line. Mixing up runs in the middle and halfback sweeps, the 'Dogs took the lead for good when Ed Barrett slipped through on a cutback play over left tackle.

After a 20–0 victory over Canton and a 74–0 shutout over Dalton, the team closed out the year by whipping Calhoun 13–0. Undefeated and outscoring their opponents 327 points to 6 points, the boys from Cedartown may have been the best in the state.

Red Lott played college football in Florida for a while and returned to Cedartown to enter the law enforcement field. In 1969, he was elected sheriff of Polk County. He gained much notoriety as a tough and determined lawman by putting a huge dent in the illegal moonshine business that ran rampant along the northwest Georgia-Alabama state line. He remained sheriff until 1974, when he was shot and killed by an unknown gunman while answering a burglary alarm at Cedartown High School.

1929

In the previous four years, Cedartown had played thirty-nine games, winning thirty-one and losing eight. Even though the 1929 team was inexperienced, Coach Lancaster believed it was talented.

Fourteen lettermen were lost to graduation, and to make matters worse, Ed Barrett lost his left arm in a hunting accident. However, Ed kept up his good spirits and declared that he would be back the next year. In the meantime, he would contribute to the team by covering the game as sportswriter for the newspaper. Ed's prowess as a writer added an extra

The 1929 Bulldogs, with Ed Barrett lined up at quarterback directly behind center. *Courtesy of Larry Carter.*

frill to the excitement of the games. His penmanship is present in the first game against Calhoun. The game was a big struggle until Paris broke through the line and blocked a punt that rolled into the end zone and was recovered by Russell for the first "marker."

Here's Ed's call of the game: "Then a little later Simpson intercepted a pass and said, 'Come to sweet papa,' and then gently folding his arm around the ball ran forty yards to the one yard line where Van Zandt, halfback for Calhoun tackled him. From this point Davis bucked it over into the land of milk and honey where the beautiful flowers bloom."

In the 0–0 game against Tallapoosa, Barrett wrote:

> *Cedartown picked to win over Tallapoosa, did not. Intercepted passes and fumbles marred the game all afternoon.*
>
> *Only in the second period did the Bulldogs show their teeth and growled, but Dickerson carried the ball over into the promised land only to fumble and this was Cedartown's only chance to score.*
>
> *Sweat streamed down young faces, hands trembled—hands clinched and shook in the air and voices yelled, "Come on Cedartown!"*
>
> *Crap-shooters talking to the dice of fate for a seven as Cedartown hasn't lost a game on the local field in three years.*

When Cedartown beat Dallas 6–0, Barrett wrote: "Out of a maze of wild and wooly footballing came the Dallas Terrors to crush the Cedartown Bulldogs' hope for another championship last Friday and to take their place at the class in the mad scramble for the Seventh District gridiron supremacy, but by the end of the game the Terrors found themselves trailing 6-0."

After Cedartown's 13–0 loss to Chickamauga, Barrett wrote:

> *Unlashing an offense that worked like magic and a defense that was hard to penetrate the Gamecocks overbowled the Cedartown Bulldogs here last Friday to the tune of 13–0. The Bulldogs were still suffering from the defeat at the hands of the Rockmart team and it seemed like they had strings tied on them—they just couldn't get going.*

For the 0–0 tie with Dalton, he wrote:

> *A magnificent and heroic team came into its own here last Thursday as the Cedartown Bulldogs completely out-played the strong Dalton team but lacked the punch for a knockout.*

It was no galloping charge of the Four Horsemen of the Apocalypse but it had a Scriptural flavor just the same. When the blood-sweating Bulldogs started fighting they longed for the taste of blood. The Bulldogs made twelve first downs to Daltons one. This fact alone tells which team fought the hardest. The game was played on a muddy field. The ball kept falling all during the game.

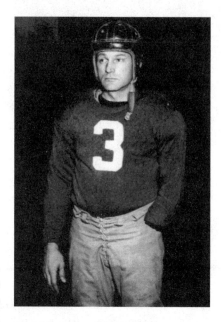

Ed Barrett. *Courtesy of Doc Ayers.*

In numbers of wins and losses, it was a disappointing year for the Bulldogs, but as far as measuring heart and determination, this team played with as much intensity as any Cedartown team. With most of the players returning for the next year, the Bulldogs believed that the winning tradition would soon return, along with halfback/sports reporter Ed Barrett.

CHAPTER 4

ENTER A COACHING LEGEND

1930

As the country faced the greatest economic crisis in history, life went on in Cedartown. Although the jobs, money and food began to dwindle, CHS was determined to put its best players on the football field. The biggest change for the Bulldogs occurred when Coach Lancaster put away the whistle and welcomed new coach Lloyd Gray.

It had been a while since the Rome Hilltoppers and the Cedartown Bulldogs crossed paths, so everyone was in great anticipation of the renewed rivalry. The Hilltoppers were well known for their aerial show and, as expected, filled the air with footballs, but it was Cedartown's quarterback, Pat Simpson, and halfback, Ed Barrett, who controlled the airways as Cedartown crashed the mighty Romans 14–0. Simpson completed a thirty-yard touchdown pass to Travis Leslie, and Earl Dickerson ran the ball over from the one to produce the second score.

The story of the game was the comeback of Ed Barrett. The one-armed Barrett caught five of Simpson's passes for over sixty yards and intercepted six of Rome's passes. He also broke up several of Rome's pass attempts and ran kickoffs back for more than fifty yards. His performance in this game brought him national attention, including a page in *Ripley's Believe It or Not*. It may be the best single-game performance of any player in the history of Cedartown football.

In the next game, Cedartown used a balanced attack to slip by a very tough Dalton team 13–6. Dickerson, running inside, set up sweeps for Milton Paris and Barrett. Simpson continued his accurate passes and tossed a twenty-yard strike to Paris for the Bulldogs' first score. Simpson connected for the extra point, and it was 7–6 in Cedartown's favor at the half. Late in the game, Cedartown was driving when an errant pass was intercepted by Dalton. Four plays later, Dalton returned the favor by snapping the ball over the punter's head. "Lightning" John Veal recovered on the five, and three plays later; Edgar Henderson went in on a quarterback sneak to preserve the victory.

The 1930 team rolled through its entire schedule without a loss to set up the Seventh District showdown with the once-defeated LaFayette Ramblers. LaFayette's only loss was to the Rome Hilltoppers. Following is the article covering the game, as written by D.W. David, manager for the Cedartown Bulldogs:

> *Lafayette Hi broke forth with a big line and a referee to defeat the Bulldogs 33–7. The referee being essential cog in the rather dubious success.*
>
> *Lafayette had a good team but not a bit better than the Bulldogs. C.H.S. with a different referee would have defeated them. Lafayette was unbeatable last week with that referee. Alabama couldn't have beat them. The referees easily gained the most yardage of the day's performance, penalizing the Bulldogs.*

Eight wins and one loss on the season gave Coach Gray a very successful beginning as head coach of the Cedartown Bulldogs.

1931

In 1931, Coach Gray had the task of rebuilding his team. Two weeks of conditioning camp in Tallapoosa and two weeks of football practice convinced him that this team was as talented as any he had ever coached. Coach Gray said, "They are as long winded as an eagle and quick as lightning, tough as a pine knot, and as cooperative as a Cadillac." The *Cedartown Standard* news story went on to make a plea to the citizens of the town to come out and help the team in spirit and financially. Coach Gray experimented with his players at different positions. He always pitted the first team against the undersized second team. His comparison of the two teams: "The second team fought like true Bulldogs, completed some nice passes and made some good tackles, but the first team is as strong as The Rock of Gibraltar. It was like a pine tree falling on a mouse."

As the season began to wind down, with tough losses to Calhoun and Carrollton, it looked as if Coach Gray may have overestimated the team's potential.

1932

Miss Irene Redding's rendition of the alma mater was adopted as the official alma mater for CHS and is still the one sung by Cedartown students today.

By a wide majority, the students of Cedartown High voted to adopt a Code of Conduct for the students. The code dealt with things like attitude and respect for the school and fellow students and especially the way boys and girls interacted.

By 1932, Cedartown had established itself as one of the most successful teams in the state, but the newspaper still made pleas for the citizens to come out and support the team. Considering all the great players who have played in the red and black and all the great games that the Bulldogs have won against every opponent they have faced, it is hard to imagine that they seldom made enough money at the gate to pay the expenses of producing the games.

Once again, Coach Gray had a lot of players to replace. The program had fallen into a pattern of playing mostly seniors and not getting much help from the underclassmen. Boyd Tamplin was elected captain for 1932.

With four lettermen returning, the lightweight Bulldogs tied 0–0 with Cave Spring and battled a much bigger Calhoun team evenly until an errant punt from the Cedartown two-yard line rolled out of bounds at the eight. From there, Calhoun muscled it into the end zone for a 7–0 Bulldog loss.

After losing to cross-county rival Rockmart 12–0, the Bulldogs got back in the winning spirit with a win over Cartersville to set up a big game with the boys from the hills of Rome. The Rome team came out of the hills ready to play, and after one quarter of football, Cedartown would have just as soon seen them go back into those hills and never return. Three quick touchdowns in the first quarter put the Hilltoppers ahead to stay as they coasted to a 27–0 win.

Averaging 110 pounds per player, Cedartown had one of the smaller teams in the area. Coach Gray had his work cut out for him if he was going to bring the Cedartown Bulldogs back to being the dominating team it was in the 1920s.

1933

In 1933, the Cedartown school system faced a low budget and overcrowded classrooms. Some classes had 60 to 70 pupils in one room, forcing them to sit in chairs with no desks to do their work. The junior high had 425 students in a building designed for 320.

Coach Gray announced that forty boys reported for the first day of football practice. In exceptionally hard times, most people couldn't afford the $0.25-cent admission charge to see the games. The gate receipts were the only way the team had to make the money it needed to outfit the team and pay all its expenses. To make it more affordable and try to raise as much money as possible, CHS offered season tickets for all six home games for $1.50. The Exchange Club and the Kiwanis Club both agreed to have all members present for every game.

Hugh Dobbs was elected captain, and Lewis Berry was elected alternate captain. The freshman class stepped up in a big way when it demonstrated its great spirit at the school pep rally and backed up that leadership when most of the class bought season tickets. The team won most of the games with running backs W.J. Foster, Edgar Henderson and Lindsey leading the charge.

With the nation on the brink of disaster, a winning football team gave folks in Cedartown little to be happy about. This was reflected in the articles, or lack of articles, written about football in the newspaper.

1934

Under the direction of the Civil Works Administration and financed by the American Legion, the old grandstand was torn down and new bleachers were installed that could seat over five hundred people. The field was sodded for the first time and had a nice stand of green grass.

Professor Purks, Coach Gray and Professor Abercrombie promised the team that if they won all their home games, they would give them a banquet at the end of the season.

Coach Gray was looking forward to the most experienced team he had fielded since becoming the coach at Cedartown. He built his team around running backs Bill Carroll, W.J. Foster and Asa Edge, with quarterback Newell Clemmons calling the signals.

One week before the opening game with Tallapoosa, Coach Gray faced an unusual situation with Clemmons, John Tyler and Floyd Gober. The players were members of the National Guard unit and were summoned to report for training.

W.J. "Dutch" Foster missed all preseason practices with a blister on his toe that had become infected. Meanwhile, A.W. Burgdorf had placed himself at the head of the class at running back.

Clemmons returned in time for the first game against Tallapoosa and led the 'Dogs to a 25–0 win. The Bremen Blue Devils were the next victims for the Bulldogs as Cedartown pulled away 33–0. The winds were fierce for the Cartersville Purple Hurricanes, but the 'Dogs held on in a tight contest to win 12–6.

Riding the wave of a three-game win streak against no losses the 'Dogs readied themselves for another invasion from Rome. The Hilltoppers, boasting a 3-1 record, understood that Cedartown had once again loaded itself with talented football players and may have the coach who could lead them back to prominence. When the battlefield was cleared and the score was tallied, Cedartown came out the winner 12–6. For the first time in five years, the Cedartown Bulldogs were on top of the Seventh District.

Carroll, Foster and Edwin Perryman led the way as top ground gainers for Cedartown, but the big play of the game came when Dutch Foster threw a pass into the end zone. The ball slipped through the hands of Rome's defensive back and into the hands of John Sproul for Cedartown's second touchdown. In a game-saving play, Perryman ran down a Rome runner who had broken through the line and was running for an apparent touchdown.

With a record of 6-0, Cedartown prepared for one of the toughest Rockmart teams it had ever played. Cedartown received the kickoff and drove the ball to the Rockmart two-yard line, where the Yellow Jacket defense stiffened and took the ball away on downs. On fourth down, Rockmart's Garner went deep into his end zone to punt. Perryman and Foster came charging through the line to block the punt that rolled out of the end zone. Cedartown was awarded two points for the safety. In the second quarter,

Garner ran for gains of twenty and thirty yards as Rockmart drove to the Cedartown five-yard line. Cedartown's defense toughened up and kept the Yellow Jackets out of the end zone. The defenses dominated the second half, as neither team was able to get inside the twenty-yard line. In a nail biter, Cedartown won 2–0.

The final game of the season was played in LaFayette against a traditionally tough opponent. Going into the fourth quarter, Cedartown was leading 13–6 when the game was called by the referees because of fighting among spectators in the stands that had spread to the players on the field. It was an ugly finish to a wonderful undefeated season for Cedartown.

Make no doubt about it, the Cedartown Bulldog was alive and well in 1934. At the student assembly, Coach Gray was given a standing ovation. Professors Purks and Abercrombie, along with Coach Gray, hosted the 1934 Cedartown Bulldogs for a banquet at the Wayside Inn.

1935

Once again faced with the loss of seventeen of twenty-three lettermen, Coach Gray began the 1935 season in a rebuilding mode. One player he didn't lose was Dutch Foster. Elected team captain, Foster was rated one of the top runners in the area. Coach Gray knew that if the offensive line could open some holes, Dutch Foster and his Bulldogs would make a fine showing.

After the previous year's dominating performances, Coach Gray had problems finding teams to play, so he looked to an old nemesis. Marietta was more than happy to renew its rivalry with the Bulldogs. With key defensive players assigned to shut down Foster, Marietta kept Cedartown out of the end zone and handed the Bulldogs their first loss in over a year, 7–0.

Tallapoosa came at the 'Dogs with the same tactics, but Lonnie Gray broke loose for two touchdowns as Cedartown slipped away from Tallapoosa 35–25.

In the first night game ever for Cedartown, Foster and Gray gave the best performances of their careers in a 25–7 Cedartown win at Dalton.

With a string of victories and only the loss to Marietta, the Cedartown boys looked forward to the upcoming march to Rome on Thanksgiving Day. No one anticipated this day more than the Roman warriors, who looked to avenge the loss of 1934.

The game was played on a muddy field before a capacity crowd with a ball that was wet and slippery. Fumbles highlighted the first quarter. Early in the second quarter, Dutch Foster put on a great exhibition of ball carrying as Cedartown scored first. Rome tied the score in the third quarter when Gilliam intercepted a pass and ran for an eighty-five-yard touchdown. Cedartown regained the lead on a play that was described by the *Cedartown Standard* writer Roy Emmett:

> *The third quarter score was one of the most spectacular plays ever seen on a high school football field and was executed with the perfection usually accredited to college teams. Foster threw a short forward pass over the line of scrimmage to Dick Thomas who immediately lattereled to A.W. Burgdorf who raced thirty yards for the touchdown. The fourth quarter score was like-wise perfectly executed and very exciting. Lonnie Gray on a delayed end run eluded three tacklers and outran the Rome secondary for 60 yards.*

A 19–6 victory over Rome was a fitting end to an almost perfect season. Hats off to Coach Gray!

1936

Coach Gray, along with Coach Roy "Firpo" Smith and Coach Rock Blackeney, welcomed back ten lettermen to the 1936 team. One of the state's top running backs, W.J. Foster, returned for his last season. Adding to the Bulldog punch were halfbacks Dick Hogan and Herman Jenkins. Robert Lindsey took over at quarterback. Although he didn't have the game experience, Coach Gray said that Lindsey was a "real gamer" who shouldn't have any problems handling the job.

In an awesome display of punt returns, end sweeps and runs up the middle, Cedartown used three distinct teams to roll over Tallapoosa 46–0. Hogan and Lindsey had good games, and Dutch Foster reminded everyone just how good of a player he was by running around and through Tallapoosa defenders. Coach Gray credited the win to the play of linemen Luke Bridges, Raymond Watson, W.P. Williams, Floyd Gober and Pat Colquitt.

On October 9, 1936, the lights came on at Cedartown's athletic field on West Avenue for the first time. The lights were sponsored by the

Cedartown Exchange Club and opened a new era of football for fans, as they were now able to come to the games after work and not worry about the onset of darkness.

All the fanfare and ceremony must have been a distraction for the powerful Bulldogs, because when the horn sounded to end the first quarter, they trailed Cartersville 18–0. In a rush of fury, the 'Dogs fought back with the strong running of Foster and tied but missed the kick for the extra point that would have won the game.

With a tarnished record and a sore mood, the Cedartown players had to pick themselves up and get ready for the Marietta team that had handed them their only loss of the previous season. After a sluggish start, Cedartown inflicted sweet revenge on Marietta 40–0.

Against Dalton, Cedartown had the ball on its eight-yard line. Dutch Foster took the ball around the end on a sweep but found no room to run. He reversed his direction and ran three yards into the end zone, where he broke a tackle to avoid a safety. He headed back up field, broke several tackles and ran all the way into the end zone. He was credited with a 103-yard touchdown run. Cedartown won handily over Dalton 34–7.

The Bulldogs learned a lesson about being overconfident up at Chickamauga. It took a last-minute interception return for a touchdown by Foster, with Gober leading the way, to pull out the 12–6 win.

Aided by two questionable penalties on two long pass plays, Trion upset the Bulldogs 19–0. The penalties for pass interference gave Trion a first down on the ten-yard line and, later in the game, on the two-yard line. The biggest factor in the game was the tremendous size of the boys from Trion. Cedartown knocked on the door all night but could not enter the end zone.

The last home game of the season was against Rockmart, and this game was picked especially to introduce the lighting system and a loudspeaker system to all of Polk County. It was also on this night that W.D. Trippe and Professor P.E. Purks dedicated the field to Lloyd Gray. On November 13, 1936, the Cedartown Athletic Field on West Avenue became Gray Field.

In Coach Gray's last game as head coach, his 'Dogs mussed up the Rockmart Yellow Jackets 38–0. He traded his playbook for textbooks and ledgers as he began his trek into the upper echelons of Cedartown education.

CHAPTER 5

COACH ROY SMITH

1937

Taking over the helm for the Cedartown Bulldogs in 1937 was Coach Roy "Firpo" Smith. Smith had been a longtime associate of Coach Gray and was the obvious choice to lead the 'Dogs. His task was huge, but Professor Gray had left the program in good condition. Over thirty players came to try out for positions vacated by stars like Foster, Lindsey and Hogan.

In the first game, the Bulldogs took the field with the backdrop of a capacity crowd of over one thousand people tapping their feet and bobbing their heads to the sounds of the Boy Scout Drum and Bugle Corp of Troop 21. The music and the drum cadence ringing out across the lighted field added to the glamour and the fanfare of the new red and black uniforms illuminating the Cedartown sideline.

The Bulldogs answered their curtain call with a spectacular showing of football supremacy as they defeated Tallapoosa 27–0. The offensive line of John McCullough, W.P. Williams, J.D. Langley, Van Hunt and Raymond Watson, flanked by ends Glen Watts and James Harwell, led the way for backs Tom Nichols, Herman Jenkins and Lester Williams. P.A. Bond got Coach Smith's call at quarterback.

Williams shredded defenses through the first three games of the season as Firpo's 'Dogs looked to regain its place at the top of the Seventh District.

Cedartown traveled to Cartersville wanting to settle the previous season's tie. Time and time again the 'Dogs drove deep into Hurricane territory only to be denied a touchdown that would give them the ultimate victory. Cartersville's offense seldom threatened Cedartown's defense, and were very lucky to get out of the game with a scoreless tie.

Jenkins exploded for runs of twenty-five and fifteen yards before carrying the ball over on a quarterback sneak to give Cedartown a 7–0 win over Marietta. The tough Cedartown defense once again kept the opponent from nearing the goal line all night. The game took its toll on the Cedartown back, as he left early with what was determined to be bruised ribs.

With Jenkins hobbled and Chickamauga fired up as usual, Cedartown played an unusually flat game and yielded a 0–0 tie. Although they were

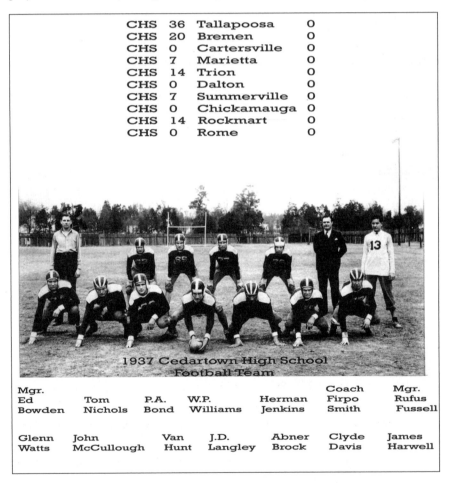

CHS	36	Tallapoosa	0
CHS	20	Bremen	0
CHS	0	Cartersville	0
CHS	7	Marietta	0
CHS	14	Trion	0
CHS	0	Dalton	0
CHS	7	Summerville	0
CHS	0	Chickamauga	0
CHS	14	Rockmart	0
CHS	0	Rome	0

1937 Cedartown High School Football Team

Mgr.					Coach	Mgr.
Ed	Tom	P.A.	W.P.	Herman	Firpo	Rufus
Bowden	Nichols	Bond	Williams	Jenkins	Smith	Fussell
Glenn	John	Van	J.D.	Abner	Clyde	James
Watts	McCullough	Hunt	Langley	Brock	Davis	Harwell

The 1937 Bulldogs didn't allow their opponents to score a single point all season. *Courtesy of Allen Hunt.*

still undefeated, Coach Smith had to be concerned with injuries that were sidelining key players.

Another scoreless tie against Dalton gave this team the identity of being unbeatable but not knowing how to win. Playing up to its full potential and looking like the power of the district, Cedartown settled the score from the last season and defeated Trion 14–0.

With a full squad of starters, Cedartown bested Rockmart 12–0 and tied Rome 0–0. The final record of 6 wins, 0 losses and 4 ties overshadows the fact that the 1937 Cedartown Bulldogs never allowed their opponents to score a single point. What a weird undefeated season. Only in Cedartown!

J.D. Langley was chosen to play in the Georgia North South All Star Game, to be played at Grant Field in Atlanta.

1938

Cedartown scheduled eleven games for the 1938 season, with some new names on the schedule. Joining some of Cedartown's traditional rivals were Russell High and Spalding High.

As the newspapers and publications lauded the great pool of talent Cedartown had assembled, someone forgot to convince the Bremen Tigers. Bremen quietly slipped into Cedartown and took a 13–6 victory over the star-struck Bulldogs. The reason given for the loss was that Cedartown was focused on the matchup with 1937 state champion Spalding High. Spalding was coming to Cedartown with a line that averaged 180 pounds and fleet-footed running backs. Giving up two quick touchdowns in the first quarter and not being able to penetrate the end zone left Cedartown on the short end of a 13–0 score.

Favored to win over Russell, the Bulldogs came out listless and let a good football team take a quick lead and never let up as Russell handed Cedartown one of its worst defeats, 58–6.

The Bulldogs got their first win of the season against Lee High of Chickamauga 25–7. This set up a duel with what some people believed to be Dalton's best-ever football team. The Catamounts' only loss of the season was against Rome 26–13. Perhaps focus was the issue for this team as it prepared for a great team and answered the challenge by beating Dalton 6–0. Wins over Trion, Rockmart and Carrollton set up the highlight game of the season against Rome.

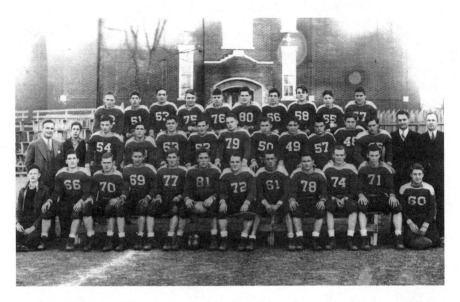

The 1938 Cedartown Bulldogs. *First row, left to right:* team manager, Lester Williams, Ed Griffin, Tom Brock, Genie Williams, Raymond Watson, Leon Tamplin, Van Wright, W.R. Rowell, Clyde Davis, Dan Carmichael, Snag Chandler; *second row:* Coach Roy Smith, unknown, Duck Dempsey, Charles Edge, Gus Murphy, Jack Sanders, C.W. Cooper, Buddy Crocker, #49 unknown, Francis Graham, #48 unknown, Buddy Peace, unknown coach, Coach Lloyd Gray; *third row:* Charles Ison, #51 unknown, #53 unknown, #75 unknown, Billy Howard, Hillary Perdue, Hook Broome, Ralph Baker, Pete Smith, Kenneth Jordan. *Courtesy of Don Smith.*

Rome's smallest player, Billy Primm, ran back a punt for a fifty-five-yard touchdown to put Rome up 6–0. Cedartown came back with Leon Tamplin passing twenty-three yards to John Teat. Tamplin threw to Lester Williams for twelve yards. Williams ran to the twenty-one-yard line, and Bond carried it in for the score. Tamplin's run for the extra point gave Cedartown a 7–6 lead. In the third quarter, Primm ran a punt back thirty-five yards and three plays later shot around right end for a thirty-yard touchdown to put Rome ahead 13–7. For the rest of the game, Rome's little elusive punt returner nullified Cedartown's long drives. Rome took home the victory 13–7 and ended a lackluster season for a disappointed Bulldog team.

1939

Coach Smith's first order of business for 1939 was to rebuild his offensive and defensive lines. With left tackle "Fatso" Watson being the only returning starter, Smith went with left guard Dan Carmichael, center Clyde Davis, right guard W.R. Rowell and right guard Ed Griffin to open the season against LaFayette. The last time these two teams played, the game was called because of fighting in the stands that erupted onto the field. Smith knew that LaFayette would be at its highest level of intensity when it visited Gray Field on Friday night. Returning running back Lester Williams and quarterback Tamplin would be joined in the backfield by Lester's brother Gene and C.V. Edge at fullback. Pass receivers Tom Brock and Ed Bruce rounded out the Cedartown starting squad. This year's starters proved they weren't going to be pushed around by overwhelming LaFayette 47–0.

As a special treat, the Cedartown Municipal Band would perform at halftime at every home game of the season.

With easy wins over Cave Spring and Summerville, the Bulldogs loaded up the bus and headed for Griffin, Georgia, for a match-up with Spalding High. The 'Dogs showed up ready to play and took the opening kickoff and drove down to the Wolfpack twenty-two-yard line before losing momentum and handing the ball over on downs. From that point on, Spalding used misdirection plays from the wing formation that kept the Bulldogs off balance and allowed them to control field position and the pace of the game. It was a tough loss for a proud and talented Cedartown team, but Spalding High had been in the upper echelons of its district for some time and showed no signs of weakening.

Cedartown beat West Fulton 36–0 and Lee High School 26–6 before it went on the road to Dalton. The Catamounts were still stinging from the previous year's disappointing loss at Cedartown and were set on revenge, but Cedartown took the opening kickoff and marched down the field for a touchdown. Lester Williams kicked the extra point through the uprights to give CHS a 7–0 lead. Dalton quickly answered when Winfred Souther broke into the open field and ran for what looked like a seventy-yard touchdown, but the referee marked the ball at the three, where he stepped out of bounds. With straight power plays, Dalton took the ball into the end zone in six plays. The Cedartown defensive line broke through and blocked Dalton's point after attempt to preserve the 7–6 lead. Late in the game, with Cedartown holding that 1-point lead, big defensive lineman Ed Griffin snatched the ball from the Dalton running back and galloped forty-two yards across the

Top: The 1938 Bulldogs: 66 Lester Williams, 70 Ed Griffin, 81 Raymond Watson. *Courtesy of Don Smith.*

Bottom: Coach Lloyd Gray with Ed Griffin, Ray Watson and Lester Williams. *Courtesy of Don Smith.*

Dalton goal line. Unfortunately, the referee ruled that the play was dead before Griffin took possession of the ball.

After a 26–0 win over Trion, the Bulldogs were expecting a visit from Soddy Daisy High School in Chattanooga, Tennessee. Soddy Daisy had apparently scheduled two games for that date and was only going to play Cedartown if the other school could not schedule Soddy Daisy. They simply informed Cedartown that they would not be attending the game in Cedartown that had been scheduled. Professor Purks announced that Cedartown would be playing another home game at the end of the season with another outstanding high school football team.

Cedartown trampled Bremen for the eighth win of the season and traveled to Rome on Thanksgiving Day as LaGrange lurked in the postseason. A record crowd of 2,500 people came out to watch Rome drop behind early and score a closing-minute touchdown to tie Cedartown 13–13. Rome coach Rufus Jennings was a happy man walking off the field after securing the tie as the Cedartown faithful felt like they had just let another big win slip away.

The linemen whom Coach Smith needed to rebuild his team dominated the line of scrimmage and opened gaping holes for the runners as Cedartown defeated a very good team from LaGrange. Big Ed Griffin, Dan Carmichael and Raymond Watson combined to give Cedartown one of its best groups of linemen in years.

The Bulldogs were declared B class champions of the western division of the North Georgia Football Association (NGFA). They were to play eastern champion Hartwell, but a suitable date for both teams could not be arranged.

1940

Cedartown coach Firpo Smith was elected vice-president of the North Georgia Football Association. Plans were being made for the Tobacco Bowl to be played on January 1 in Waycross, Georgia. The game was to be a matchup of all-stars from the B classification in the north against the stars from the south.

Western Auto and Coca-Cola teamed up to install a new public address system for Gray Field as Firpo Smith welcomed back eighteen lettermen to take on Tech High from Atlanta. Led by the steady running and passing of Lester Williams, the 'Dogs scrambled to a 60–6 trouncing of the Bees.

After a lackluster performance against Cartersville, Coach Smith decided to add more speed to his lineup by moving Lester Williams to fullback and inserting "Racehorse" James Bradshaw into the tailback position. Spalding County was coming to town, and Smith didn't believe the Bulldogs were playing the brand of football that it was going to take to beat a team that Cedartown had never beaten. Both teams were being touted as one of the best, and Smith knew that if they didn't take down the giant, the chances were very slim that Cedartown would make it to the state championship title game. Captain Charles Edge was quarterback, with Hillary Perdue on the wing behind the blocking wall of Tom Brock, W.L. Rowell, C.W. Cooper, Dan Carmichael and Ed Griffin. Gene Martin and Buddy Peace rounded out the offense on the end positions.

Twelve hundred excited fans lined the sidelines as the opening kickoff sailed into Cedartown's end zone. The Bulldogs took possession of the ball on the twenty-yard line and moved the ball to Spalding's fifteen-yard line. Lester Williams tossed the ball to Buddy Peace at the five-yard line and he ran into the end zone for the score. Cedartown's offensive line opened holes all evening for Williams and Bradshaw.

Griffin, Carmichael, Brock and Cooper lined up on the defensive side of the football and shut down the powerful Spalding running attack in the backfield before the play had time to develop. In what Smith called "the best executed game I've ever seen," Cedartown answered the question that had been posed to it by Spalding County. By a score of 25–6, the Bulldogs stated, "Yes, we can really play!"

After winning 36–6 over Lee High from Chickamauga, Dalton's Catamount prowled onto Gray Field with a screeching hiss and a powerful claw that had the old Bulldog fighting for his life. While Dalton's aggressive defense held down Cedartown's running attack, the Catamounts used a series of short passes, aided by a pass interference penalty, to claim the first score at the end of the first half. In the second half, Cedartown found cracks in the defensive line and evened the score at 6–6. The Catamounts were not finished and were soon knocking at the door. The Bulldogs stood their ground and took over the ball on the one-yard line. Three plays later, Cedartown's Arthur Perdue went back into his end zone to punt. A Catamount player slipped through on the inside to block the punt. The ball bounced out of the end zone for a safety, and Dalton was back on top 8–6.

After Perdue's free kick, Dalton set up shop on its thirty-three-yard line. After two running plays, a pass and a Dalton punt, Cedartown took possession on the forty-four. Running the ball up the middle, the Bulldogs got big gains from Perdue and Williams. Williams took the ball into the end zone from seven yards out. Williams added the kick for the extra point, and Cedartown was ahead to stay 13–6.

Firpo's 'Dogs won them all. A tough 12–0 tussle with Rome and a perfect season won them the great experience of traveling to Athens, Georgia, and playing in Sanford Stadium against Athens High for the North Georgia state championship. With four minutes to play in the game, James Bradshaw threw a twelve-yard touchdown pass to Ralph Baker to secure a 6–6 tie with Athens. Cedartown missed the kick for the extra point, but Athens was called for offside and penalized to the one-yard line. Williams tried to push it over from there and was stopped just short of the line.

The NGFA committee met and determined that a playoff between Cedartown and Athens would be played in Cedartown on December 13, but Athens did not want to prolong the season and forfeited the right to the championship. The Cedartown Bulldogs would travel to Albany, Georgia, to play the Valdosta Wildcats for the state championship on December 20.

Special permission from the U.S. Army was obtained for C.V. Stewart, James Bradshaw, Francis Graham and Charles Isom to return to Cedartown and play in the championship game. The players had recently been inducted into the army and were to be stationed at Fort Stewart near Savannah.

For three quarters, the Cedartown defense turned back Valdosta's lightning quick offense, but in the fourth quarter, the depth of the Wildcat runners proved to be too much for the 'Dogs. Valdosta scored three touchdowns in the fourth quarter to end the Bulldogs' dream of their first-ever state championship title by the score of 21–0.

This game marked the third state championship ever to be played. The first game, in 1937, was won by the Spalding County Wolfpack over the Moultrie Packers 6–0. There was no game in 1938 because South Georgia was unable to declare a champion. The 1939 game saw the Albany Indians defeat the Athens Maroons 20–0.

CHAPTER 6

RETURN OF THE SCHOOLMASTER

1941

For undisclosed reasons, Firpo Smith retired from coaching football after the 1940 season. Not able to find a suitable replacement, Lloyd Gray returned to the sidelines to take over as head coach. Matching Smith's run to the state championship game was a tall order, but Gray was a skillful tactician and a great motivator.

Gone was Lester Williams, but in to take his place was his brother, Gene Williams. Hillary Perdue returned to play fullback, and the speedy Francis Graham came on to play halfback. Joining lettermen Carmichael and Baker on the line were Arthur Nuttall, Jack Hamil, Harry West, Horace Pyle and Dick Burgdorf.

In what was becoming an ordinary occurrence, the 'Dogs had little trouble with their first three opponents. In the big game against Spalding County, Coach Gray thought that the team missed several opportunities and should have handily defeated the Wildcats in a close 6–0 win.

On Thanksgiving Day, four thousand fans came out to watch Cedartown play Rome. The Bulldogs drove inside Rome's ten-yard line six times but were only able to score one touchdown in a disappointing 7–7 tie with the Hilltoppers. By virtue of their won and loss record, Cedartown would once again play Athens in Sanford Stadium for the North Georgia championship. Cedartown never rebounded from the disappointing tie with Rome and was dismantled 36–6 by a fired-up Athens team that was out for revenge.

1942

Captain Melvin Kirkland, Leftwich Watson, Roy Brewster, Harvey York, Thurrell Smith and Joe Lanham are just a few players whom Coach Gray counted on to lead the Bulldogs in 1942. It was time to rebuild, and the old coach was wondering if he had the stock to fulfill the expectations of a fan base that was used to winning all of the time.

Under the guidance of Buford Smith, the Cedartown High School marching band made its first appearance in a parade down Main Street. That same evening, the band began its rich tradition of performing during halftime of the Bulldog football games.

Unfortunately for the Bulldogs, Rockmart brought an unusually tough football team to town and scrapped with the Bulldogs until the final whistle sounded for a 0–0 tie. Before Coach Gray could right the ship, Spalding County had gotten into the fray, handing the 'Dogs their first regular-season defeat in more than two years.

In a game that was called the best game ever played on Gray Field, Cedartown prevailed over its newest rival, Athens High. The game was played to a dead even tie after three quarters, but midway into the fourth quarter, Matt Ware escaped on a reverse and raced forty-five yards for the score. On Cedartown's next possession, they drove the ball down deep into Athens territory, and Harvey York scored on a sweep to give Cedartown the 12–0 victory.

Just when it looked like the Bulldogs were on the right track and steamrolling for another championship season, they were derailed in Trion. In a game that was as lackluster as the Athens game was exciting, the 'Dogs could never get the offense on track. With a chance to tie the game, Ralph Baker fumbled the football just before he crossed the goal line. Trion upended the Bulldogs 7–0.

A Thanksgiving Day 27–6 loss to Rome put an end to a tough but interesting 1942 season.

1943

Charting familiar waters, Coach Gray began the 1943 season with forty players but only six with playing experience. Gray remembered all too well his early years, when Cedartown fell into a pattern of continuous rebuilding.

Recognizing that he had talented players who were just starting to develop gave the coach plenty of encouragement. He predicted that the team would be competitive and fun to watch as the Rockmart Yellow Jackets prepared to invade Gray Field. Pedro Meyers, Matt Ware and Harvey York all scored touchdowns as the Bulldogs broke up a defensive battle in the second half to defeat Rockmart 23–6.

New stars began to emerge in the next game against Atlanta's Boys High as Jack Hamil and Frank Thomas stymied the offense from the right and left defensive tackle positions in a 12–0 Cedartown win. Fans were all in agreement that Hamil's performance was one of the best defensive performances they had seen in some time.

Spalding County proved to be a most unwelcoming host when Cedartown visited for a game that was turning into an annual grudge match. Spalding waxed the Bulldogs 20–6. The 'Dogs fought hard, but the Wolfpack was loaded with upperclassmen who had a distinctive edge on the younger Bulldogs.

Athens High didn't roll out the red carpet when it saw the 'Dogs coming and sent them packing with a 35–6 shellacking.

After pounding Rockmart 65–13, Cedartown prepared to host the 1942 defending state champion, Griffin Gold Wave. Griffin came into the game undefeated and hadn't given up a score all season. The only positive report on that game for Cedartown was that it was the first to score on Griffin as it went down 33–6.

Beating Marietta 27–13 and Dalton 21–13 set up the annual Thanksgiving showdown with Rome. The final score of 12–6 left Cedartown with a record of five wins and four losses. Coach Gray knew he had some young, talented players and that better days were ahead.

1944

Don Smith was elected captain of the 1944 team, which got off to a fast start by winning the first three games. In the fourth game, the 'Dogs relied on big plays from the defense to come from behind twice and tie Spalding County 12–12.

In the matchup with cross-state rival Athens, Cedartown broke open a close game that was tied at the half and rode out of Athens the 32–13 winner.

Taking their undefeated record on the road to Griffin, the Bulldogs had the ball on the one-yard line when the first half ended with the score Griffin

6, Cedartown 0. In the second half, bad luck and costly mistakes allowed Griffin to score two quick touchdowns and put the game away 19–6.

The Bulldogs went into the Thanksgiving Day classic with Rome boasting a record of eight wins, one loss and one tie. It didn't matter much to the Hilltoppers because they continued their recent domination of the Bulldogs 19–6.

1945

In August, Coach Gray attended a football clinic in Atlanta that was hosted by Georgia Tech. Instructors of the clinic were Wally Butts, coach of the University of Georgia Bulldogs; and Bobby Dodd, coach of the Georgia Tech Yellow Jackets.

Back home in Cedartown, fourteen lettermen waited anxiously to put on the red and black uniforms and take the field. Gray knew that this class was special and loaded with workhorses like Homer Roberson, Dave Roberson, Don Smith, Billy Carter, Dick Philpot, Charles Pickard and Fairfax Mullen.

Decisive victories over Commercial High, Atlanta's Boys High and Newnan led to the showdown with Spalding County. Led by the running of Fairfax Mullen and Tommy Hunt, the Bulldogs broke a 0–0 halftime tie and defeated Spalding County 12–0.

The next week, Wally Butts and the University of Georgia Bulldogs were the guests of honor as Athens High hosted Cedartown at Sanford Stadium. Athens and Cedartown had been building a rivalry since they first met in the North Georgia championship game in 1940. Cedartown fumbled the opening kickoff to set up Athens's first score. The 'Dogs came roaring back down the field to get even when Billy Carter took a reverse twenty-seven yards to the two-yard line. From there, Charles Pickard took it in on a quarterback sneak. Cedartown took the lead when Tommy Hunt connected with Don Smith for a forty-one-yard touchdown pass. The 'Dogs went up by two scores when Harley Lee took a reverse into the end zone from thirty-two yards out. To seal the victory, Hunt connected with Reed Fitton for a twenty-one-yard score. Athens scored another touchdown late, but it was the Bulldogs all the way, winning 28–20.

The next team on the schedule was the formidable Griffin Gold Wave. The 'Dogs had never beaten the Gold Wave, but the winner of the game had the inside track to the North Georgia championship. Cedartown scored

The 1945 Bulldogs. *First row, left to right:* John Henry Blackwell, Frank Thomas, James Veal, Joe Paris, Dave Roberson, Homer Roberson, Kensin Brannon, Joe Byrd, Hugh Hardison, Tommy Hunt; *second row:* Fairfax Mullen, Charles Pickard, Reed Fitton, Ray Beck, Herman Pyle, Willie Perkins, Fen Martin, Red Baxter, Harley Lee, Don Smith; *third row:* Coach Lloyd Gray, Charles Hamrick, Dewey Hamrick, Billy Carter, Carl Linderson, Adams, Jimmy Hamilton, Dickie Philpot, Coach W.B. Thomas; *fourth row:* Charles Roberson, Van Brewster, Joe Brewster, unknown, unknown, Bill Bruner, Hubert Adams, Douglas Burgdorf. *Courtesy of Don Smith.*

first when Carter made a big run to get the ball into Griffin territory. Mullen lofted a pass to Brock Hamrick, who was brought down at the goal line. From there, Dave Roberson carried it into the end zone. Griffin fought back with a series of plays that consisted of multiple laterals and scored to tie the game. The Bulldogs bounced back to take the lead when Hunt ran the kickoff back to the forty-three-yard line. He then threw a long pass to Hamrick for the score.

Griffin took the second-half kickoff and drove the ball the length of the field, relying on good upfront blocking to make gains on runs and short passes. The extra point was missed, and Cedartown led 13–12. Hunt and Carter carried the workload as Cedartown moved the ball to Griffin's twenty-seven-yard line. Again it was Hunt and then Carter moving the ball to the four-yard line, where Dave Roberson carried three times to break the plane of the goal.

Dave Roberson, Cedartown football running back, Golden Gloves boxer, sportswriter and friend in the community. *Courtesy of Greg Roberson.*

With the clock winding down, Griffin punted the ball out of bounds at the Cedartown one-yard line. Not wanting to take a chance on a bad play or poor snap from center, Cedartown elected to punt on first down. A Griffin lineman broke through the line and deflected the kick. The ball rolled out of bounds on the ten-yard line. Cedartown's defense stiffened and held Griffin to three incomplete passes and one short run. The ball went over to Cedartown, and the clock ran out with the Bulldogs driving in Griffin territory.

The next week, the band accompanied the Bulldogs as they traveled to LaGrange. Hundreds of people lined the streets as the band marched in a parade and then put on a pre-game concert. The Bulldogs had their backs against the wall for the entire first half holding off LaGrange drives that carried them inside the ten-yard line. The first half ended in a 0–0 tie with LaGrange at the Cedartown four-yard line.

Cedartown received the second-half kickoff feeling a little less pressure and was able to flex the offense. After an exchange of punts, Tommy Hunt broke loose over right tackle and raced eighty yards for the first score of the game. LaGrange fumbled on the next possession, and Cedartown recovered on the twenty-seven-yard line. Hunt and Homer Roberson carried the ball in from there to put the 'Dogs ahead 13–0.

In the fourth quarter, LaGrange's quarterback raced thirty-three yards on a sneak. A completed pass moved the ball to the eight-yard line, where the halfback carried the ball in to keep them in reach. Mullen passed to Hamrick at the LaGrange thirty-four-yard line. Three plays later, Tommy Hunt tossed a lateral pass to Carter, who carried the ball the distance to seal the 20–6 victory for Cedartown.

Marietta rolled into Cedartown and rolled out not knowing what hit it as Cedartown clobbered the old rival 64–0. With an easy victory over Trion and then against Rockmart, the 1945 Bulldogs ended the regular season undefeated. By virtue of Cedartown's won-loss record and wins against all the major teams in the North Conference, they were declared North Georgia champions and would play Thomasville in the sate championship game in Albany.

The Cedartown businessmen arranged for a Central of Georgia train to leave Cedartown at 4:00 a.m. and arrive in Albany at 12:30 p.m. so that the cheerleaders, the band and local fans could travel to Albany for the game. The train would leave Albany at 6:30 p.m. and arrive back in Cedartown at 2:00 a.m. The cost for the tickets was $11.21 for adults and $5.24 for children. Total cost for the train was $1,680.80. The local businessmen agreed to pay any difference between the cost and the ticket sales.

As a record crowd of over six thousand fans looked on, Cedartown took an early first-quarter lead. Thomasville roared back with a safety and a quick touchdown to take the lead and was never threatened. It was a long, unhappy train ride home. The untold story is that because of pneumonia and influenza, several Cedartown players didn't make the trip. Some who did were not able to play their best football. It was a bitter ending to another great football season by a great football team. In the six-year existence of the state championship game, Cedartown represented North Georgia twice.

Lloyd Gray turned in his playbook for the last time after the 1945 season and became a full-time school administrator. He eventually became the superintendent of schools and retired with over thirty years of dedicated service to the Cedartown school system.

CHAPTER 7

KIMSEY, WALLER, LUCK AND BOULWARE

1946

Coach Gray stepped aside in 1946 and handed the reins to Cliff Kimsey. Just as he had done for Firpo Smith, Coach Gray left the locker room full of talented football players. Veteran utility player Billy Carter led a group of skilled players. Tommy Hunt had become one of the state's premier running backs. Ray Beck and Dickie Philpot were becoming outstanding linemen on both the defensive and offensive sides of the ball. Cedartown was one of the favorites to return to Albany for the state championship game.

After downing Commercial High, the 'Dogs once again stumbled against Bremen. They retuned to the win column with a record-breaking 502 yards and seventeen first downs against Trion. Billy Carter intercepted a pass and returned it to the two-yard line to set up the win over Spalding County. Wins over Athens, Griffin, LaGrange and Marietta set up a showdown with powerhouse Decatur High. The 13–13 score was a moral victory for the Bulldogs.

The only team standing between Cedartown and a playoff game with Gainesville was the undefeated Rockmart Yellow Jackets. The Yellow Jackets had not allowed any opponent to score more than one touchdown. Nearly 6,500 fans lined the field to watch the Yellow Jackets score late to take the 13–6 victory. Rockmart defeated Gainesville but lost to Cairo in the championship game. Tommy Hunt was named to the first team of the NGFA All-State Team.

1947

Coach Kimsey left after one year, and Wylie Waller brought his two-year record of 17-3 from Cartersville to Cedartown. The season began with a tie against Bremen. Scoring on a safety and a fumble recovery in the end zone, the 'Dogs beat R.E. Lee 8–7 without scoring a touchdown. Despite having players like Ray Beck, Dickie Philpot, John McCarson and Floyd Wilkes, the Bulldogs could only salvage two wins and two ties in a disappointing season.

Ray Beck and Dickie Philpot. *Courtesy of Doc Ayers.*

1948

Jim Luck had a little bit more success than the previous two coaches. After he won the first six games, people began believing the team had turned things around and was back to the winning ways. A 7–6 loss to Griffin seemed to take its toll on the team, as the 'Dogs could salvage only one win in the second half of the season.

Dickie Philpot was given a scholarship to play football for Vanderbilt.

Ray Beck went on to become an all-American football player for Georgia Tech and was inducted into the College Football Hall of Fame. In 1952, the New York Giants drafted him into the NFL. He served in the U.S. armed forces during the Korean War and returned to the Giants in 1955. He was a member of the Giants' 1956 NFL championship team.

1949 AND 1950

In 1949, the Cedartown team continued its downward spiral. After salvaging four wins, Jim Luck may have found the climate a little bit too cool in Cedartown, because he left for the warmer weather of Americus, Georgia.

Ben Boulware had just completed two very good seasons at Gordon Lee and was chosen to lead the team into the next decade. After winning one game and losing nine, Ben was more than happy to take a head coaching job at Chattanooga Valley.

CHAPTER 8

CALL HIM "DOC"

1951

He came in late August 1951, which was a little bit late to be starting a new football program. He wasn't the first man called to take over the Cedartown program. John Bell had come up from Americus to take over the program but decided that Americus and Jim Luck needed him more than Cedartown. He said that he would feel guilty if he didn't return to Americus as an assistant. One man's junk is another man's treasure, because Howard Ayers didn't hesitate when Lloyd Gray called and offered him the job.

They called him "Doc," but he didn't carry a medical bag or wear a stethoscope around his neck. What he did have was a playbook, a whistle and a blue ribbon recipe for molding high school boys into football players and men. He says it was for the money, but once you look into the heart of Cedartown High School, you realize that he came because he knew he was needed. He had a no-nonsense approach to discipline that required his players to do their best on the field, in the classroom and in the community. He led by example and defended his program on every challenge. He went right to work, and before long, he realized that he had a group of kids who hustled and gave 100 percent. Doc may have been the one who coined the phrase "110 percent."

When Doc named his captains, he picked linemen Alton Gilmore and Bobby Broome and fullback Gene Simmons. It was a good group of youngsters who stepped up and showed great leadership and sportsmanship.

Right: Howard "Doc" Ayers, coach of the Cedartown Bulldogs and freshman coach for the University of Georgia. *Courtesy of Doc Ayers.*

Below: Doc Ayers's first captains: 34 Gene Simmons, 22 Alton Gilmore, 31 Bobby Broome. *Courtesy of Mr. and Mrs. Alton Gilmore.*

His first quarterback was Eddie Barrett, son of Ed Barrett from the 1928, 1929 and 1930 teams. Robert Baxter was the center. Bradley Clinton and Ed Wilkes were the halfbacks. The ends were Floyd Brock, Bobby Ellenburg and Ed Fowler. Anchoring the line of scrimmage were Jimmy Hanson, Billy Joe Banks and Bobby Lindsey.

The first team up to test Doc's mettle was the always-tough Rossville Bulldogs. Everyone who saw the game witnessed a Cedartown team that was full of fight. They kept it close and threatened to take the lead until Rossville gained control in the final quarter and defeated the 'Dogs 25–7.

West Fulton, Marist, Dalton, Marietta and Griffin were teams in Georgia's highest classification and probably the toughest in the state. Cedartown played them all, and although the 'Dogs didn't win, they served notice that no longer were they going to be the doormat of northwest Georgia. Players like Charles Ivie and Ed Wilkes were hard-nosed runners. Against Marist, Ivie returned a punt fifty-six yards for a touchdown. With a sluggish offense and stubborn defense the 'Dogs kept it close but were unable to take the win.

The next week, Griffin High jumped out to a 6–0 lead when Wilkes hauled in a punt on his own eight-yard line and scrambled ninety-two yards for a touchdown. Gene Simmons picked off a Griffin pass and went eighty-one yards for a touchdown that put Cedartown in front 13–12. With the Bears leading 19–13, the Bulldogs drove down to the Griffin twenty-four-yard line before time expired, ending the chance of pulling off the home field upset. Although they weren't winning, the bunch from Cedartown played with tenacity and emotion.

Finally, on November 2, Doc and his 'Dogs got their first win against Cartersville, 12–6. The next week, Cedartown jumped out to a 12–0 halftime lead over Rome only to see the Hilltoppers come back and win 20–12.

In the last game, the Bulldogs welcomed the Rockmart Yellow Jackets to an overflow crowd at Gray Field. The 'Dogs led early and kept up the heat as they ran away from Rockmart 40–6. Written in the 1952 Cedartown yearbook: "A wonderful ending to an enjoyable season!"

Looking through the sports section of the annual yearbook, Doc Ayers is pictured as a football coach, a basketball coach and a track coach. Along with his assistant coaches, Lester Williams and Ralph "Red" Simmons, Athletic Director Ayers fielded teams for baseball, track, tennis and golf. The leading golfer was Doug Sanders, who went on to become a famous professional golf player.

Realizing the need to build for the future, the three men fielded junior varsity teams in football, basketball and baseball. They laid down the foundation of hard work and dedication by their actions, not by their words. In every picture on every page of the yearbook, the smiles and happy faces of both the boy and girl athletes show how much they enjoy playing sports. A picture tells a thousand stories, and the most important message coming from these pictures is that Doc had a very successful first year as head coach and athletic director.

1952

The next year, when summer practice came around, Doc loaded up the team and traveled to Hard Labor State Park in Rutledge, Georgia, for summer football camp. Hard Labor is exactly what it was, as the boys came back lean and mean. After two weeks of beating up on one another, they were anxious to butt heads with the real enemy.

That real enemy came in the form of one of Cedartown's toughest foes. The 'Dogs were going to get a grand test, as they opened the season with Rossville. Coming off a season in which they won only two games, this bunch of 'Dogs was determined to right the ship and steer the CHS football team out of rough waters. Everyone on the team remembered the whipping that Rossville had put on them the previous year and marked their calendars for the first Friday in September. It was a hard-hitting battle as the defenses dominated. With determination and desire, Ed Wilkes took control of the offense and began running over Rossville defenders. His kickoff return from the five-yard line to the Rossville ten set up the winning score for a 14–6 Cedartown victory.

Cedartown wanted to ride the wave of momentum in the second game against Dalton. Both defenses dominated the game. Cedartown got its only touchdown when Eddie Barrett passed to Floyd Brock at the ten-yard line. Floyd turned and pitched a lateral pass to Ed Lindsey, who ran it in for the score as Dalton and Cedartown settled for a 7–7 tie.

After a big win against Russell High, Spalding County brought its squad to Cedartown. After four quarters of hard-hitting football, the two teams settled on a 19–19 tie. The big loss for Cedartown was losing captain Guy Womack to a season-ending injury.

The next week, the 'Dogs went on the road to face a very tough Decatur squad. Decatur flexed its muscles and handed CHS its first loss of the season, 34–20.

Three more wins against Marietta, Summerville and Cartersville had the Bulldogs riding high heading into the matchup with Rome. Cedartown led throughout the contest, but Rome fought back and took the lead with only seconds remaining in the game. A riot broke out that ended the game. Doc said he was only concerned with getting his team off the field and away from the trouble.

November 24 marked the debut of the Cedartown Midget football team that was coached by Don Smith and Ed Brewster. The Midgets had been limited to a couple of intra-squad games before they played West Rome to a

6–6 tie. These boys were the teams of the future for the Doc Ayers program and many programs to come.

The season came to an end as Cedartown defeated the region 3A champion Rockmart Yellow Jackets. The Jackets showed their stinging power, but the Bulldogs were too big and too strong as they took control in the fourth quarter and won 20–6.

Guy Womack was selected to the Georgia all-state team.

1953

In August 1953, the Bulldogs traveled to South Georgia for summer camp at Kolomoki Mounds State Park in Blakely, Georgia. Coach Ayers wanted the boys to experience new places and discover new and interesting things like the Indian mounds. Doc put the team through rigorous workouts, but a visit from Cedartown citizens and players' parents revealed that Kolomoki was more like the Waldorf Astoria Hotel with its cozy lodging and delicious food.

Football is a sport of controlled violence where swinging forearms and elbows sometimes result in players losing teeth. On the 1953 team there were several defensive players who had lost at least one tooth while playing football. These fellows banded together and called themselves the "toothless five." This tough group of players led a Cedartown team that was the most talented that Coach Ayers had put on the field. Don Williams, Douglas Barrett, Charles Edwards, Mike Knighton and Ski DeArman flashed their bright smiles that exposed missing teeth to the yearbook photographer.

The team returned to Cedartown ornery and sore, with two major goals. The first one was to beat Rossville, and the second was to win the region championship. In Rossville, a pouring rain limited both teams to running the ball. The game ended in a 0–0 tie. Only in a game on the home field of a dreaded rival could a scoreless tie be considered a victory.

Undaunted, the 'Dogs went on to pound Dalton 20–7. Ranked fourth in the state and anticipating a barnburner from top ten–ranked Griffin, the Bulldogs got no less as the Bears mauled and clawed their way to a 19–0 win.

The next week, Decatur was waiting at the gates of Gray Field to tag Cedartown with a 14–0 shellacking. The tailspin continued the next week when the short trip to Marietta proved to be a long ride home after a 6–6 tie. It was nothing like the jubilation of the ride home after the tie with Rossville.

Marietta was half the distance that it was to Rossville, but the ride home seemed to take twice as long.

The next week was a long journey to play Baker High in Columbus, Georgia, that resulted in another loss 6–12.

Finally, the team regained its composure and finished out the season with wins over Rome, Cartersville and Rockmart, which brought the end to less than what was expected that season.

Doyle Broome was selected to the Georgia all-state team.

1954

In 1954, the CHS football team won four games and lost six. There is a photograph in the 1955 yearbook where Doc Ayers doesn't look very happy. Why should he be? After all, he had arranged for the team to make a trip to the Florida coast to play a team from Panama City, Florida. For most of the players, it was the first time they had ever seen the ocean. He took them out deep-sea fishing and gave them the experience of a lifetime and a lasting lesson on how to recover from being seasick. Perhaps there was too much play and not enough work for this team. Or maybe it was time to rebuild. After progressing for three straight years, Doc had lost a lot of his seasoned veterans. The team was in transition and needed some time for solid players to emerge.

The season began on a sour note with a 13–0 loss to Rossville. It was just as sour after an identical loss to Dalton. With subsequent losses to Russell, Griffin and Decatur, the five-game losing streak had become downright bitter. A true test of the integrity of the Cedartown fabric was on the line, and everyone watched to see if the team would fold. They proved their mettle when a tough Marietta team came in wanting to deliver the final knockout punch that would have put the lights out on the '54 season. The mighty Bulldogs got off the mat and slugged it out for a 7–0 victory.

With a win to their credit, the 'Dogs went on a four-game winning streak but hit a brick wall when they traveled to East Polk County and nearly upset a Rockmart team that had only one loss and wouldn't lose again until it played Jesup for the state championship.

1955

After building some momentum from the late-season turnaround and the town still buzzing about the thriller against Rockmart, everyone looked forward to a successful 1955 season. Doc brought in former NFL lineman Herb Hannah to coach the offensive line. It looked as if the 'Dogs were going to regain their winning ways when they opened up with a win at home against Dalton. A tough loss at home against Russell set up a road loss at Griffin. It was obvious that the Bulldogs were struggling to find ways to put away the opponent and kept settling for a loss. Every game was close, but more times than not the final outcome went in favor of the opponents. This team had size, speed and strength, but to win consistently in Georgia's highest classification against quality teams that had just as much heart and desire wasn't going to happen every year.

Four pages, eight photographs and no captions are all that was devoted to the team in the 1955 yearbook. The managers, Jerry Durham and Bob Powell, were commended for wrapping ankles, carrying dummies and working as hard as the players. Doc's photograph was beginning to look ominous. Maybe he knew or maybe he didn't know if better days were just around the corner.

Herb Hannah left Cedartown after one year. Both of his sons had successful NFL football careers. Lloyd Gray Jr. tells a story about five-year-old John Hannah falling down the steps at Purks Junior High. As the youngster began to cry, his dad picked him up and instructed him to apologize to the team for crying in front of them. John went on to become an all-pro lineman in the NFL. In 1981, *Sports Illustrated* named him the Best Offensive Lineman of All Time. In 1991, he was inducted into the NFL Hall of Fame. Herb and John were both well liked by the Cedartown players.

1956

In 1956, Bill Keller came in to coach the linemen. A kid named Jerry Weaver stepped up and demanded a chance to play quarterback. He was too short, too slow and couldn't throw the ball more than thirty yards. Coach Ayers asked him what he could do. He responded by saying that he could outrun any player on the team running backward. Jerry's father had instructed him to work on running backward because quarterbacks ran backward to set up and pass.

Coach Ayers nodded at the tires he had assembled for practice and asked Weaver if he could throw the ball through a tire. His father had also given him some very strict workouts in passing accuracy by demanding that he throw a ball through a dangling tire without ever missing. Weaver quickly picked up a ball and whisked it through the tire. Doc asked him how many times he could do that. Weaver responded that he could do it as many times as he wanted. Doc gave the junior quarterback his chance, and it paid dividends for the team.

The undersized quarterback Dusty Mills had inspired Weaver when he watched Mills lead the south all-stars to victory in the 1956 all-star game. Knowing that Cedartown had graduated twenty-nine players from the previous season's team, Weaver believed that this was going to be his best chance to win the quarterback job. Once he took over the play-calling role, he excelled as a passer and a leader. Game after game he marched the offense down the field, throwing passes to Mink Wilson, Wayne Hill and Van Tanner. He had a host of running backs like Jimmy Vincent and Tommy Andrews who were capable of gaining huge chunks of yardage running between the tackles. Halfbacks Lawrence Wilkes, Wendell Jones and Freddie Clinton could break long runs sprinting around the corners. Opening up holes in the line of scrimmage were linemen Don Edge, Dave Woodward, Harry Tracy and Bobby Bates.

At the beginning of the season, Ayers believed the team was too young and too inexperienced to compete for the region championship. By late in the season, he was commenting on how his team was rich with talent.

One by one, the opponents lined up to face the mighty Bulldogs and were defeated. There was one blemish in an otherwise perfect season when they were declared the winners by penetration in a 14–14 tie against Dalton when they won the 4AAA North championship.

Decatur was the only team standing between Cedartown and Doc Ayers's first region championship. Decatur jumped out to a 20–0 halftime lead, and Doc had to do something fast. According to Jerry Weaver, Doc gave one of his most brilliant halftime performances when he reached inside his coat pocket and pulled out a letter. It was a letter that Doc's mother had written to the team to explain to them why she was not at the game. She said that she hadn't missed a game since Doc had become the coach but that she had fallen and hurt herself and was not able to attend. She wanted the players to know that even though she wasn't at the game, she was with them spiritually and would be praying for them throughout the game. When he finished reading the letter, Doc looked up with tears welling up in his eyes. He said nothing as he walked through the door and back onto the field. Some of the players had tears running down their cheeks as they jammed the doorway trying to get on the field and get back on with this game. Another former player says that Doc had dropped the letter. It was picked up by one of the managers. When he looked at it, he saw that it was a blank sheet of paper. He stuffed it in his pocket and never said a word about its lack of content. The Bulldogs came storming back to win the game 26–20 and were the 1956 4AAA Region Champions.

Quarterback Jerry Weaver returned to Cedartown to practice medicine until he retired. *Courtesy of Dr. and Mrs. Jerry Weaver.*

The next week, Waymon Creel brought his undefeated Northside Tigers to Cedartown for the North Georgia championship. A dream season came to a sad ending as the Tigers took away the 'Dogs' hope for a state championship by a score of 20–0.

Don Edge, Mike Knighton, Jerry Weaver, Lawrence Wilkes and Jimmy Beecham were named to the Georgia all-state team.

1957

High school football teams are in a constant state of building and rebuilding. A boy begins his high school development at the age of fourteen or fifteen and doesn't reach his peak until after he is out of high school. A team's maturity is determined by the timing of the players' development. An ideal team consists of mostly juniors and seniors with a few sophomores working hard to earn playing time. The remainder of the sophomores and most of the freshmen are grouped together to form a junior varsity team that competes in the region against other junior varsity teams. Usually, great teams surface when they have a lot of seniors who are near their peaks and are supported by upcoming juniors who are at nearly the same potential. The hard-hitting sophomores, who are hungry for playing time and a chance to make a name for themselves, challenge the upperclassmen.

From time to time, a little phenomenon occurs when the junior class progresses quickly and takes leadership of the team. The seniors are still prevalent, but there exists one or more juniors who step up and take over leadership roles in positions like quarterback or running back. When this happens, great teams seem to suddenly emerge and upset a lot of teams. Sometimes these teams of underclassmen make great accomplishments and even win championships. With most of the starters returning for the next season, expectations are high, and anything less than a championship is a disappointment.

This was the scenario of the 1957 team that followed the 1956 4AAA Champions. Returning were star quarterback Jerry Weaver, halfback Tommy James, fullback Bud McCreary and receiver Mink Wilson. Sixteen seniors were to lead the Bulldogs in their quest to repeat as region champions and, hopefully, go on to win the state championship. Along with a first-class team came a first-class schedule, with teams like Marietta, Southwest Dekalb and Marist not wanting to be pushovers for this new dog with a big bite. Cedartown was in the state's highest classification, playing against teams that were well funded and loaded with talent.

The first week, the 'Dogs traveled to Habersham County and won a close 13–7 victory. The next week's trip to Marietta for a region contest was disappointing, as Weaver and company could not find the end zone and made the long ride home after the 13–0 loss.

Perhaps too much sulking and not enough preparation led to a disappointing 13–7 loss to Marist. Now the senior-laden team that had only lost one game the previous year stood with two losses and only one win with Rome waiting on the hill.

It probably wasn't a pleasant ride up highway U.S. 27 on Friday evening as the Bulldogs traveled to visit an old rival. Doc knew his team was better than the 1-2 record and was ready to set them straight. When great teams have their backs up against the wall, they rely on their defense to pull them through. By stacking the line of scrimmage to shut off the run and sack the quarterback, Cedartown held Rome to 58 yards rushing. The offense finally got back on track and ran the ball for 186 yards and passed for 87 yards as the Bulldogs returned to the winner's circle with a 21–0 win over Rome.

The win streak went on until it was briefly interrupted in Panama City, but the 'Dogs got back on track in the next game with a 19–0 win over Dalton.

The next week, undefeated Avondale jumped out to a two-touchdown lead. Weaver passed twenty-five yards to Wilson to close the score to 13–7 going into halftime. Taking the second-half kickoff back to the forty-yard line, the 'Dogs drove sixty yards to tie the game. Weaver went back to pass for the extra point and was under great pressure. He threw an out-of-control pass toward Mink Wilson, who out-leaped three Avondale receivers to put Cedartown ahead for good.

The undefeated Rockmart Yellow Jackets brought a disappointing season to a close, thumping the 'Dogs 28–12. Rockmart put together a fine season, losing only to Athens in the state Class A championship.

1958

Losing a total of twenty-two players from the 1957 squad put Coaches Doc Ayers, Bill Keller and Lester Williams back into a rebuilding year. Nevertheless, the table was set, and as the saying goes, "winners begat winners." Small kids who were in the bleachers when Doc came to town were now in high school and were anxious to try out for the team that had been making the news all over the state. When the team boarded the bus for Kolomoki Mounds, Doc had the most players ever on his football team.

Despite losing the opening game to Newnan, the 'Dogs stormed back to win five straight before losing to a very good Bay County, Florida team. Wins over Calhoun and Dalton set up a big game with an old nemesis, Rossville. Although they played them tooth and nail, Rossville came away with a 16–13 win. The Bulldogs' record was good enough to make them sub-region champions and put them back on the heels of Rossville. The Bulldogs from the north reclaimed their dominance by winning 20–6.

Co-captains Lloyd Gray, Dickie Astin and Buddy Stephens led the team. Eddie Brewster called the signals and passed to receivers Dudley Lentz, Jerry Moore and Phil Carter. Running backs Stephens, Gary Price and Carter amassed 1,812 yards running the football.

Great plays that were recorded by the CHS yearbook were Bill Haney's sixty-seven-yard punt return against Darlington, Buddy Stephens's eighty-three-yard kickoff return against Sprayberry, Jerry Moore picking up a fumble and returning it eighty-eight yards against Rossville and Dickie Astin stopping East Rome's Pat Moss at the goal line. One remarkable thing about the players of this team was the way they adopted the strut of the Cuban gamecocks. Doc had lectured to his team about the quickness of the Cuban gamecock. Chicken fighting was still an acceptable sport on the international level, and some of the toughest fighting chickens came from Havana, Cuba. Doc described the Havana rooster as a fast, tenacious and deadly killer that flapped its wings and strutted around its prey, just as the Cedartown Bulldogs displayed their version of the Cuban gamecocks as they strutted off the field after stopping West Rome on a fourth down and three.

This team made great accomplishments in a rebuilding year and looked forward to returning a lot of players the next year.

1959

This team was not about to disappoint anyone and, except for a slight stumble against East Rome, would have gone undefeated. After putting away that pesky Rossville, the 'Dogs avenged themselves by shutting out the Gladiators of East Rome 27–0 in the sub-region championship game. Unfortunately, the next week Rossville dished out its own brand of revenge when it downed the 'Dogs 20–6.

Returning players Ed Brewster, Ronnie Dollar, Phil Carter, Jerry More and Gary Price led a team that Doc described as "the most dedicated group of young men I have ever coached."

Only East Rome scored more than one touchdown against them in the regular season, while Cedartown scored as many as fifty-three points against Sprayberry, allowing Doc to empty his bench and let everyone play in the second half.

Finally, Doc Ayers had established a football tradition in Cedartown that was beginning to automatically rebuild itself. Young boys sitting in the bleachers were dreaming about becoming a quarterback like Jerry Weaver or running the ball like Ed Wilkes, but more importantly, they just wanted to be Cedartown Bulldogs. Midget Football had been giving the youngsters an introduction to football before they were old enough to play football in junior high school. By the time they reached high school, they knew the plays, the formations and the cadence of the varsity team.

All was well with the Cedartown football program, but Doc realized that the job was not finished and wouldn't be complete until Cedartown wore the crown of the state champion. No matter how many great players and great games a program plays, it is still marked by the number of championship teams produced. Nobody knows that better than Howard "Doc" Ayers.

1960

Establishing a program that has a tradition of winning and pursuing the state championship is every coach's objective. Falling short of that elusive title has left many good football teams in the shadows of obscurity. So it may be with the 1960 team that had tough losses to Newnan and Rossville, but it was the one-point loss to LaFayette that turned the season into a disappointment. Rossville went undefeated until it lost in the state semifinal championship game to Gainesville.

It was certainly disappointing to seniors, but this team was loaded with juniors and sophomores who had moved in and claimed their positions. They were the nucleus of great things to come.

One was none other than the son of the coach, Bucky Ayers. Installing his son at quarterback in his sophomore season opened the coach to a lot of scrutiny. Doc would later say that he had been harder on Bucky than any other player he ever coached. Doc had earned the respect of the citizens of Cedartown, but he encountered some criticism from people questioning if Doc was being too hard on the youth.

1961

Laced with size, strength and speed, the 1961 Bulldogs had high hopes and lofty goals. Co-captains Joe Kines, Jimmy Norris, Larry Odom and Dennis Vincent led a group of hard-hitting seniors who were determined to make it all the way to state. Doc had already raised the brow of the local fans when he installed his son, Bucky, at quarterback, but it didn't take long for everyone to realize that young Bucky wasn't in there for the glory. He was in there to perform, and Doc wasn't going to settle for less than perfection.

It wasn't long, however, until the old "rock in the shoe," Rossville, showed up and edged out the 'Dogs 13–12. As all Doc Ayers teams do, they regrouped and went on a 6-1 run to close out the season as 3AA sub-region champions. Once again, the Bulldogs would have to face Rossville for the region crown. In a battle of giants, Rossville pulled out the 10–7 win and went on to the state finals, where it was beaten 23–7 by Waycross.

Initially, Joe Kines was a walk-on player for Jacksonville State University before earning a full scholarship. After college, he coached football at the college and professional levels for forty-four years. He was known as a great communicator who loved football and his players.

1962

There's an old saying used to describe someone of an undesirable nature who is always coming around to be "turning up like a bad penny." This is in reference to back in the days when a penny was actually worth something and getting stuck with one that was counterfeit was an undesirable situation. In the case of the Cedartown Bulldogs, that bad penny was the Rossville Bulldogs. If there were ever any arguments as to who had the toughest dog or which dog was on the longest chain, those arguments could have been won by Rossville. Rossville's presence was no more prevalent than it was in 1962, when Cedartown's only two losses came against the 'Dogs from the north end of Georgia's Highway U.S. 27. That was all it took to unravel an otherwise perfect season for the 1962 version of the Bulldogs. The feeling after the second loss was gut wrenching for Doc and his staff, which had now grown to include Lloyd Culp, Ray Carter, Lester Williams and Max Bass.

In 1962, the 'Dogs won nine games and lost two. Along the way, they beat every team in their sub-region. They beat Bay County, Florida, but could not get past Rossville, losing by one extra point in the regular season and then by two extra points in the region playoff.

Early in the first quarter of the first game, Rossville quarterback Paul Painter faked out everyone in the stadium when he faked a handoff up the middle, tucked the ball into his hip and ran around right end for a sixty-seven-yard touchdown. The kick for the extra point made the score 7–0 in favor of the northern Bulldogs. Painter also doubled as the punter and kept Cedartown pinned down deep in its own territory for the entire first half. The best starting field position for Cedartown in the first half was the twenty-six-yard line.

After an exchange of fumbles deep in Cedartown territory, Painter hit a low line drive punt that Bucky Ayers caught on the run on the Cedartown forty-seven-yard. Ayers faked a handoff to running back Miller and ran down the left sideline for a fifty-three-yard touchdown. Running the option play that would have given Cedartown a 7–7 tie, Ayers pitched the ball to halfback Steve Shiflett, who was smothered inches from the goal line. The rest of the game was a defensive standoff, as neither team threatened the opponent's goal line. Coach Ayers said that the teams were very closely matched, and it is not often that all the scoring in one game comes off two plays.

Cedartown ran through the remaining schedule with little trouble and was anxious to get another shot at Rossville in the region championship game.

Rossville boasted a 10-0 record and was ranked No. 1 in both writers' polls. Cedartown finished the season at 9-1 and was ranked No. 2 in one poll and No. 5 in the other. An overflow crowd of five thousand packed in to Gray Field to see the rematch of two of northwest Georgia's finest football teams.

The Bulldogs from Cedartown set the tone for the game and put themselves on the defensive when the fullback fumbled the ball on the first play from scrimmage. Capitalizing on the momentum, Rossville drove the ball fifty-two yards in nine plays. The kick for the extra point was good, and Cedartown trailed 7–0 early in the first quarter.

The 'Dogs from Cedartown proved to be up to the task and came storming back with an eighty-three-yard touchdown drive. Once again, they came up short on the run for the extra point.

Coach Ayers had added a couple of new twists to his option offense that kept Rossville off balance for most of the evening. Behind Bucky Ayers's passing and Shiflett and Jerry Turkett's running, Cedartown moved the ball easily through the Rossville defense.

Rossville wasted no time bouncing back. After two running plays, Painter lofted a pass just out of defender Jimmy Carter's reach for an eighty-seven-yard touchdown. Rossville was back on the scoreboard with a 14–6 lead.

Ayers and company took control of the ball on the thirty-four-yard line. Set up by Shiflett and Turkett making hard runs up the middle and Tony Wiggins making quick sweeps around the corner, Ayers drilled a long pass to Elliott Gammage, who fell down on the one. From there, Ayers ran the ball off tackle into the end zone. The extra point was good, and Cedartown trailed 14–13.

Rossville received the kickoff to start the second half and couldn't move the ball, so they had to punt. Cedartown received the ball on its own forty-five-yard line. Fifteen plays later, Bucky Ayers scrambled out of the backfield on a quarterback draw and ran fourteen yards to put Cedartown ahead 19–14.

Late in the fourth quarter, Rossville had a fourth down with one yard to go at midfield. The Cedartown linemen buried the Rossville fullback, but once again, Painter bootlegged the ball on his hip and ran around right end for the first down. Finally, the drive stalled, and Painter went back to punt. Playing it safe, Ayers let the ball roll out of bounds on the Cedartown six-yard line. Trying to give themselves room to punt and run some clock, the 'Dogs ran one play up the middle. Then Ayers scooted outside to gain five yards. On third down, Shiflett drove into the line and pushed with all his might to get a first down that would have secured the region championship—until a hand slipped in and pulled the ball loose. Rossville recovered on the fourteen-yard line. The Bulldogs toughened up and tried to deny the canines from the north another score, but with three minutes and thirty-two seconds left, Rossville went into the end zone to make the score 21–19.

Ayers and company took the field in a race against the clock. Davidson ran for nine yards and Shiflett for seven yards, followed by a pass to Gammage for nine yards. Then Shiflett got sixteen yards on the option play. A fourteen-yard pass to Gammage gave the 'Dogs the ball on the nine-yard line with fifty seconds left in the game. Ayers sneaked for two yards, and then Shiflett ran for five yards. With eight seconds to play, Ayers threw a pass out in the left flat to Shiflett. When pressured by the defense, Shiflett pitched the ball back to Ayers. When Ayers was stopped at the line of scrimmage, he handed the ball off to Pounds, who ran into the end zone for the apparent score.

The referees said that Ayers's forward motion had been stopped and did not allow the touchdown. Both benches and the stands emptied onto the field as arguments raged. A few scuffles broke out, but no one was hurt. Finally, things settled down, and Rossville was declared the winner of the game and region 3AA Champion.

In the statistical category, Cedartown had sixteen first downs to Rossville's eight. They ran the ball for 139 yards, compared to 125 for Rossville. The Bulldogs from Cedartown dominated the airways, as Ayers passed for 113 yards to Rossville's 67 yards. Losing in only one category (the final score), Cedartown was left at home to lick its wounds while the Rossville Bulldogs went on to win the AA state championship with a record of 13-0.

Bucky Ayers running the football against Rossville. *Courtesy of Doc Ayers.*

Coming off a stellar season, Lynn Gammage and Bucky Ayers were named to the Georgia all-state team. Bucky Ayers was named the *Atlanta Journal-Constitution* Back of the Year as he passed for over one thousand yards and ran for over five hundred yards. Pitching in workman-like numbers was Steve Shiflett, who caught thirty passes for over five hundred yards and ran for five hundred more. Gammage, Ayers and Shiflett played for the North All-Stars in the 1963 Georgia North versus South All-Star Game. The South Stars won the game and were coached by Jimmy Hightower, who in later years was a one-season coach for Cedartown. The Bulldogs had a sensational year that had all the ingredients of championship football but came up a couple points short. Doc said he was so close to a championship that he could "taste it."

1963

Going into the 1963 season, Doc wondered how he could improve on the previous year's team. Three points between Cedartown and the eventual state champions were all that kept his team from being undefeated. Sure, with only a sub-region championship to its credit there was plenty of room for the team to improve, but with the loss of his entire backfield and other key starters, he knew his team had a rough road to travel. If he held a somber mood entering summer camp, it was quickly expelled when he saw the development of players like Edgar Chandler and Elliott Gammage. When he witnessed the sleek-handed ball handling of his new quarterback, Jimmy Carter, a ray of sunlight emerged as his team took on a competitive nature. The previous year's subs had grown up and filled out. They were anxious to get the new season started.

The offense had shaped up to be quick and versatile. Carter was becoming a proficient passer and tough ball carrier. He also revealed a strong leg for punting the football. Opening up holes in the line were tackles Edgar Chandler and Jimmy McClendon beside guards Chuck Bunn and Roy Blankenship. Jerry Turkett was the power runner from the fullback position, while the halfbacks were Tony Wiggins and Scooter Stephens. All-state prospect Elliott Gammage would anchor the tight end position as speedster Steve Barrett played split end.

Doc's most pleasant surprise came when he discovered that Turkett and Mark Knighton had become more than good linebackers—they had become "headhunters." The fierceness they brought to the defense began to rub off on other players. When Chandler and Gammage stepped into the fray, suddenly Cedartown had one of the most tenacious defenses in Doc Ayers's tenure as head coach.

As quickly as the sun came out, a dark cloud made its way onto the horizon when Gammage broke a bone in his foot. He would be out for several weeks, and it was doubtful that he would be ready to play in the first game in Newnan. Chandler had not fully recovered from knee surgery he had over the summer and was also questionable for the first game. Doc began shuffling people around in the lineup and bringing in new faces. With each addition to the scheme, another player emerged. Stepping in behind Chandler were Russ Edge, Paul Doss and Bobby Ramey. Olin Hackney and Jabby Brock added depth to the tight end position. On game day in Newnan, Doc knew that this team had some unresolved issues, but he also knew that he had brought a busload of boys who were ready to play football. They did not let him down.

Scooter Stephens shredded the Newnan line that had been softened by Jerry Turkett's hard running in the middle. Jimmy Carter ran the offense with the coolness of a three-year starter. The defense was solid and became impenetrable when Doc brought Edgar in to play defensive end. He moved Steve Barrett to the other defensive end and brought Carter in to play safety to stop two Newnan drives deep in Cedartown territory. Two scores by the offense were more than enough as the "Doggone" defense pitched a shutout.

Revealing his own razzle-dazzle, quarterback Carter faked a handoff to Stephens and bootlegged around right end for a touchdown. His fake was so convincing that the referee whistled the ball dead when Stephens was tackled. Although the Cedartown coaching staff protested vehemently, the ball was placed on the twenty-eight-yard line. Three plays later, Carter ran the same play into the end zone for the first score of the game.

After easily disposing of the East Rome Gladiators, that gnarly dog from Rossville showed up at Gray Field boasting a fourteen-game winning streak. Doc called his troops together for his pre-game pep talk and told them that the fair was coming to Cedartown on Monday and was bringing a wrestling bear. Doc said that if they beat Rossville, he would get into the ring and wrestle that bear. They believed him, and when they hit the field with such ardent force, Doc believed they just might pull it off and beat Rossville. It wasn't to be because the defending state champions had returned most of the starters from the previous year's undefeated season. A key play in the game was when Tony Wiggins fumbled the football in Rossville territory early in the second half. Otherwise, Wiggins had a memorable night, making several long runs and catching two passes. One run that he nearly broke for a touchdown went for thirty-nine yards. It didn't matter about the bear, because when the fair came to Cedartown, there was no wrestling bear.

The 'Dogs returned to their winning ways against Calhoun, but the next week, an ailment overcame the team as it suffered from a serious case of "fumbleitis." Cedartown fumbled the ball eight times and lost six of them against Chattooga and narrowly escaped with a 13–12 win. The condition improved the next week when the Bulldogs shut out the West Rome Chieftains 20–0.

No one knows if the LaFayette Ramblers were really that good or if Cedartown was looking forward to its annual trip to Panama City, Florida, but what is known is that the Ramblers nearly succeeded in ending all of Cedartown's championship hopes. The news that Dalton had upset reigning champion Rossville could have figured into the formula. Doc Ayers stated that all the defensive and offensive schemes were sound, but the boys did not execute them accordingly. Nevertheless, after a 12–12 tie, Cedartown was not in control of its own destiny, and the sub-region champion could ultimately be decided by a coin toss.

The next game in Panama City, Florida, witnessed one of Cedartown's worst offensive performances in years. Lester Williams said it was the worst since 1952. The 'Dogs played the Tornados to a 0–0 deadlock for the first half, but the storm blew in and blew out the Bulldogs 20–0.

If someone had predicted that Cedartown's win-loss record after eight games would be five wins, two losses and one tie, Doc Ayers would have probably agreed with the prediction. Even after the drubbing that Bay City High put on it, Cedartown was still on top of the sub-region, and a championship run was still a possibility. This was not the time for Doc to lose focus or get after his players for not putting forth the effort. The coaching staff continued to drill the players as usual, and things settled down in time for the game against Northside Warner Robins, and the Bulldogs drilled the Eagles 39–0. The news traveled quickly from LaFayette that the Ramblers had lost to East Rome and that Cedartown was the south region champ. One more victory over Rockmart and the showdown with Dalton was set.

Dalton came into the region championship game with a 9-1 record, having lost only to West Rome. More important was its victory over Rossville. This was the first time in years that Rossville did not stand between Cedartown and a state championship.

Cedartown put its mark on the 1963 season against Dalton in the first quarter with a touchdown on the opening drive. The score was set up when Jimmy Carter returned the punt from the Cedartown thirty-five-yard line to the Dalton thirty-nine-yard line. With Turkett pounding the middle for long gains and Carter bootlegging around the corner, the 'Dogs led 7–0 early in the quarter. After Dalton failed to move the ball and punted out of bounds, Cedartown was in business again at its thirty-five-yard line. Carter passed over the middle to Barrett for thirty-three yards. On third down, Carter threw a pass downfield to Gammage, who fought off two Dalton defenders and fell down on the two-yard line. Then, like a flip of a switch, the momentum swung in the other direction. A poor exchange from the center to the quarterback sent the ball rolling free on the turf. Dalton's Jimmy Weatherford recovered and kept Dalton in a game that seemed to be in Cedartown's control.

Late in the second quarter, when Carter was back to punt, the center's snap was off the mark, causing Carter to hesitate his kick. Once again, it was Weatherford who came charging in to block the kick. The ball rolled into end zone, just out of reach of the Dalton defenders and out of bounds. A safety was called, and Dalton was awarded two points. Cedartown made a hasty attempt to score in the waning seconds of the half. A long pass to Olin Hackney moved the ball to the Dalton twenty-yard line, where Carter missed a field goal as time expired.

Cedartown played its best defense of the year in the second half and didn't allow the Catamounts to get any closer than the forty-four-yard line. The game ended when Carter took the snap from center and downed the ball. Cedartown prevailed 7–2 and was 1963 3AA Region Champion.

The Baldwin Braves were big and tough. They were the biggest team Cedartown had played all year, and they were set to come into Gray Field and push the 'Dogs around. They did just that for the first quarter and took a 6–0 lead, but Cedartown turned the tables and shut down Baldwin 41–6. Steve Barrett led the way with two touchdown pass receptions and one touchdown run. One remarkable play was when Ronald Peek blocked a pass, caught it and ran it in for a touchdown.

So it went. Carter passed the ball, Turkett and Stephens ran it, Wiggins and Barrett caught it, but it was the defense that dominated the game and allowed North Clayton one long desperation pass for a score. The dream season finally came true for Coach Doc Ayers, who thirteen years earlier had taken over the program that no one really wanted and turned it back into a perennial power and eventual state champion.

Right: Edgar Chandler, perhaps the most beloved Bulldog of all time. *Courtesy of Polk County Historical Society*.

Below: Bucky Ayers (10) and Jimmy Carter (26) shown with teammates and Coach Ralph "Shug" Jordan of Auburn University. *Courtesy of Doc Ayers*.

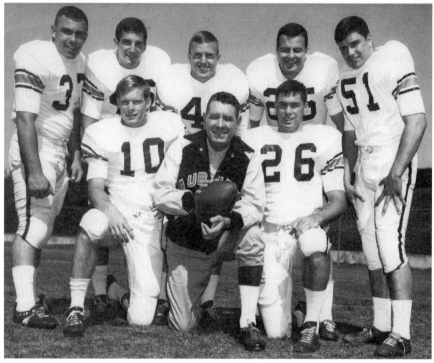

Joe Williams, *Cedartown Standard* news editor, wrote, "Cedartown High parlayed a sizzling air game and a dirt-digging defense Friday night in Jonesboro to wallop North Clayton, 21–7, for the first state AA football championship in Bulldog history."

Jimmy Carter was named to the *Atlanta Journal-Constitution* all-state team. He played college football for the University of Auburn, where he was an all-SEC defensive back.

Edgar Chandler was named state Lineman of the Year. He went on to become an all-American at the University of Georgia and played several years in the NFL. He is perhaps the most beloved Bulldog of all times.

Rumors began to swirl about Doc leaving Cedartown to become a coach at Auburn, where Bucky had signed to play. He denied the rumors but turned heads when he was the first coach hired by Vince Dooley when he took over as head coach of the University of Georgia. Doc coached for Georgia for nineteen years and is now a semi-retired chaplain for a law firm in Cedartown. In 1991, Doc and Ray Beck formed the Doc Ayers and Ray Beck Community Foundation. Every year, the charitable organization sponsors the Doc Ayers–Ray Beck Celebrity Golf Tournament in Cedartown to raise money for local charity organizations.

CHAPTER 9
FOUR COACHES IN TWELVE YEARS

1964

The Cedartown Board of Education raked through dozens of applications for the new coach at Cedartown. All the assistant coaches were qualified applicants. After much deliberation, the board decided to give the job to Assistant Coach Ray Carter. Carter, a Cedartown native, joined the staff after graduating from Jacksonville State in 1957. He started out coaching the junior varsity football team and the junior varsity basketball teams. In 1961, he moved up to coach the varsity linemen, as well as the varsity boys and varsity girls basketball.

The only assistant who remained was Lloyd Culp. Jim Mayben, who played quarterback at Alabama and Jacksonville State, was hired to coach the backs. Melvin Crook, a letterman lineman from the University of Georgia, was brought in to coach the linemen. Doc's longtime assistant, Lester Williams, took the head coaching job at Elbert County. Max Bass went to Bolles High School in Florida for a short stint and returned to Georgia to coach Newnan High for twenty-nine years.

Although players like Edgar Chandler, Jimmy Carter and Elliott Gammage would be hard to replace, Coach Ayers hardly left the cupboard bare. The 1964 Bulldogs would certainly be revealing some new stars to go along with seventeen returning starters. Just as the 1963 team had to rebuild its starting backfield with journeymen Carter, Wiggins, Stephens and Turkett, the '64 team was looking forward to a season of excitement with super speedster

Dickie Chandler moving up to take the leading role of running back. Chandler stood five feet, seven inches tall and weighed 135 pounds, but he was as quick as a cat and as fast as the wind. Jerry Whitton and Joe Brewster were set to battle for quarterback, but Brewster up and moved to Florida to play for Max Bass. David Morgan and Mike Lemming would compete for fullback as Dennis Sutton and Jerry Holder vied for the other halfback position. The offensive and defensive lines returned experienced linemen Allen Rhinehart, Dennis Gann, Bobby Shiflett and Russ Edge. Jabby Brock and Dwight Jolly were solid at the end positions.

A packed house of 3,500 fans came out to support the first showing of Ray Carter's 'Dogs. Moving up to class AAA, Cedartown was considered the underdog against the AA Newnan Tigers. To make things more difficult, Dickie Chandler had a nagging injury and would be held back to limited action, if he played at all. It was an intense atmosphere as Cedartown's defense dominated the Newnan offense. On the other side of the ball, the Bulldogs killed every drive with turnovers or untimely penalties. In the end, it was the foot of Pete Astin and hustle of Dwight Jolly that set up the only score of the game when Astin made a tremendous punt of fifty-four yards that Jolly downed six inches from the goal line. On fourth down, Newnan's center snapped the ball over the punter's head and rolled out of bounds for a safety, giving Cedartown a 2–0 victory. Ray Carter left the field knowing well that it would be a tough night at home the next week against Rossville if his offense continued to turn the ball over on miscues.

Rossville came into Cedartown with a focus on not being left out of the state playoffs again. The previous year's one loss to Dalton was enough to eliminate it from a chance for back-to-back championships. Most teams would boast that a season of nine wins and one loss was a great season, but for Rossville, it was a major disappointment. Like Ray Carter, new coach Lynn Murdock had some big shoes to fill at Rossville. He had his team fit, fresh and focused when it stepped onto Gray Field on Friday night. As Hurricane Dora sent her mighty winds and storms through Cedar Valley, the Rossville Bulldogs released a lightning-quick force in 140-pound Eugene Dupree. Dupree returned a first-quarter punt down the sideline for a sixty-yard touchdown, and Rossville dominated the Bulldogs 25–7 on a sloppy Gray Field.

On week three, the Bulldogs traveled to Marietta to play Sprayberry High. Sprayberry jumped out to a three-touchdown lead in the first half. Cedartown battled back in the second half with long drives but was only able to cross the goal line for one score. A sore shoulder was still bothering Dickie

Chandler, but he showed flashes of his tremendous breakaway potential with several runs over ten yards. He finished the game with fifty-eight yards on twelve carries. David Morgan continued his steady production with forty-eight yards on twelve carries.

Coach Carter pointed out certain deficiencies on the line of scrimmage that prevented the Bulldogs from taking advantage of Sprayberry's weaknesses. He served notice to his players that from this point on the most productive players who were better at executing the plays would be the players on the field, even if it meant playing on offense and defense.

Traveling to Rome to take on the East Rome Gladiators turned out to be a big disappointment in the final score, as East Rome took advantage of key Cedartown turnovers to grunge out a tie and nearly pick up the upset. Although Carter was unhappy with the final outcome, he had high praise for the play of his linemen.

The next week, the 'Dogs got back on the winning track with a 31–6 win over R.L. Osborne.

Wanting to improve the passing game, Cedartown passed the ball twenty-eight times against South Cobb. Jerry Whitton completed sixteen of those passes for 164 yards. Dwight Jolly caught seven passes for 94 yards. Dickie Chandler rushed for 76 yards, and David Morgan ran for 31 in a game that ended deadlocked at 7–7. Cedartown's defense was terrific as it kept South Cobb from crossing midfield most of the night. Miscues, penalties and turnovers plagued the Bulldogs every time it looked like they were going in to score. Cedartown coaches were pleased with the effort and the overall play of the entire team.

Going into week seven with a 2-2-2 record wasn't exactly what Coach Carter was looking for, but he would have to take it. After all, it wasn't a losing season, and with big games coming up against West Rome and Bay County, Florida, there was still a chance to turn things around. Unfortunately, it didn't happen. Once again, turnovers, along with stalled offensive drives, proved to be the Achilles' heel for the 'Dogs. Add that to the hustle and the speed of the Chieftains' Dickie Sapp, and Cedartown departed Rome after losing another game that it should have won. This was one of those games where the home team felt like it was playing twelve players. On several occasions when the 'Dogs tried to break Chandler loose on corner sweeps, there was one extra man in a black-and-white striped uniform out there who forced him to run wider than usual. Having to run around the referee allowed the Chieftain defenders time to catch up to the speedy ball carrier before he could cut up field. It was a frustrating night for the Bulldogs, but they had better regroup quickly because there was a storm brewing in Florida.

There was turbulent weather down in Florida, but it wasn't a hurricane dousing barrels of water onto the field. It was the Bay County Tornadoes ripping through the Cedartown defense and demolishing the Cedartown offense in a 33–7 blowout. Making this long trip to take a beating like this one was beginning to become more of a nuisance than a pleasure to Carter and the Bulldog staff. It was the last time Cedartown scheduled or played Bay County High in Panama City, Florida. The final tally was Cedartown five wins and Panama City six wins.

After a close win over Rockmart, Cedartown finally played up to its capabilities with a 39–14 win against Campbell of Smyrna.

Allen Rhinehart and Dickie Chandler were named to the 1964 *Atlanta Journal-Constitution* all-state team.

1965

If Doc Ayers turned heads when he started his son Bucky at quarterback, Ray Carter sent them spinning when he sent ninth grader Wendell Rhodes in to replace the injured John Ayers in the first game against Newnan. Carter liked Rhodes, and quarterback coach Jim Mayben liked him. To this day, Jim Mayben says that Wendell Rhodes was the best high school quarterback he has ever seen. As a freshman, Rhodes stood six feet and two inches tall. He was an accurate passer and possessed the strongest arm that had been seen around Cedartown for a long time, if ever. Rhodes responded with a fifty-four-yard touchdown strike to Dickie Chandler as the Bulldogs rolled to a 27–7 win over the Newnan Tigers. Mike Lemming led the way, rushing for eighty-eight yards as Chandler added seventy-seven yards. Carter was quick to hand out praise to his backs and to defensive player Dennis Gann. He noted in the *Cedartown Standard* that Gann and Lemming each had eight tackles. This game also marked the varsity debut of Frank Burgess Jr. The sophomore defensive player had also shown great potential running the football out of the fullback position.

The spirit and momentum didn't last long, as the 'Dogs ran into a haymaker in Rossville, falling 27–0. Things began to unravel a bit more when Sprayberry came to town and put a 28–7 thumping on Carter's 'Dogs.

To give the team a spark and unleash one of his powerful weapons, Carter installed Rhodes as his starter in game three against East Rome. The team responded by beating the Gladiators 14–8. Chandler thrilled the hometown crowd when he took the opening kickoff straight up the middle for a ninety-four-yard touchdown run that took exactly ten seconds off the clock.

Against South Cobb, the Bulldogs staged a mighty comeback to tie the Eagles 14–14.

Cedartown limped into the next game against West Rome at Barron Stadium. This was supposed to be a grudge match and a chance for the 'Dogs to pay back the Chieftains for the previous year's game—a game that Cedartown felt it should have won. On top of the injuries, several players were either out or recovering from the flu. West Rome's record was 2-4-1, but it was a different team after Coach Paul Kennedy made several personnel changes.

The Chieftains went ahead 6–0, but Cedartown came back to score and make the extra point, giving the 'Dogs a 7–6 lead at the end of the first quarter. West Rome went ahead 13–6 on a score that was set up by a halfback pass. Cedartown never threatened in the second half, and the Chieftains pulled away for the 26–7 win. This game meant more than just a win for West Rome. It also gave the Chieftains the inside track to win the sub-region. Two weeks later, West Rome defeated the East Rome Gladiators to become the sub-region champ and went on to win the 1965 AA State Championship with a 7-5-1 record.

In his next game against Wheeler High, Dickie Chandler ran the football for 241 yards with touchdown runs of 91 yards, 55 yards and 20 yards.

Cedartown closed the season with wins over Rockmart and Campbell of Smyrna to finish the season at 6-3-1.

Dickie Chandler and Dennis Gann were named to the 1965 *Atlanta Journal-Constitution* all-state team. Chandler went to the University of Alabama on a track and field scholarship.

Cited by Carter for his great defensive play, Ray Woods was named permanent co-captain. After high school, Woods enlisted in the U.S. Army and was killed in action in Vietnam.

1966

After two years at the helm of Cedartown High School, Ray Carter had a combined record of ten wins, seven losses and three ties. Considering the region Cedartown played in and the level of competition it played each week, a .575 winning percentage was commendable. Not everyone expected Coach Carter to come in and repeat as state champions, but losing two years in a row to a West Rome team that had never beaten the 'Dogs gave local armchair quarterbacks reason to be concerned about the direction the team was heading. No doubt the Chieftains were the eventual state champs, but a lot of folks believed it should have been Cedartown waving the championship banner. Season three would be a big test for Carter and his Bulldogs. Gone were the players who had been developed in the Doc Ayers years. Every starter from here on out would be the product of Coach Carter and his staff.

Things looked pretty bright for the Bulldogs at the quarterback position with Wendell Rhodes's strong arm and John Ayers's ball handling and running ability. Another bright spot was the emergence of Frank Burgess Jr. at fullback. Frankie had done his homework and handled all his assignments well. Burgess was a bruising inside runner with deceptive speed once he broke into the secondary. Danny Grimes and Joe Edge were beginning to look capable of replacing the dynamic duo of Dickie Chandler and Mike Lemming. Ends Butch Pierce and Carey Atkins rounded out the offensive threat. The linemen could be the core of the team with returning seniors Russell Jolly, Mike Elliott, Grady Teems, Gary Hackney and Bill Woodruff. Pushing those big guys for playing time would be junior Ty Johnson and sophomore Tommy Beck. Joe Rentz, Sammy White, Chip Roberson and Mike Baker would battle for the center position. Coach Crook was busy deciding who would get the draw for the offense and who would be better suited for the defensive side of the ball. The report coming out of camp was that this year's group was the hardest-working and most enthusiastic group that these coaches had brought to camp.

Senior John Ayers was selected by the coaches to open the season at quarterback for the 'Dogs. He responded by gaining 133 yards on nine carries as the Bulldogs' defense stopped Cartersville on several drives deep in Cedartown territory. Junior Danny Grimes flashed Dickie Chandler–type speed as he broke off runs of 58, 38, 35 and 2 yards for 133 yards. Cedartown ran the football for 398 yards as it defeated the Cartersville Purple Hurricanes 19–14.

Carter warned everyone that the LaFayette Ramblers were always a tough game for Cedartown. Even though they had lost the first game of the season, LaFayette had always played tough against Cedartown, even playing to a 27–27 tie in the Bulldogs' championship season.

Coach Jack King of LaFayette employed what could be called a flex defense that allowed Cedartown to have short minimal gains by spreading out his defense. As they backed closer to the goal line, he pulled his players up to the line of scrimmage to stop even the short runs. His scheme worked to perfection, as Cedartown gained 194 yards in the first half but was only able to cross the goal line once. A missed extra point put the 'Dogs ahead 6–0 at intermission.

The second half was much like the first, with Cedartown mounting long drives that stalled deep in Rambler territory. In the fourth quarter, with just under two minutes to play, Cedartown was trying to run out the clock but fumbled and turned the ball over on the LaFayette thirty-eight-yard line. On second down, LaFayette quarterback Chapman threw a desperation pass just beyond the reach of the Cedartown safety and into the arms of substitute receiver Bill Cross. Cross bobbled the ball but was able to gain control and ran untouched for a sixty-two-yard touchdown. The kick for the extra point put LaFayette ahead to stay 7–6. Coach King said that Bill Cross had not caught a ball in a game or in practice all year long. For Cedartown, it was a bitter pill to swallow.

"Get up and shake it off" is the motto for athletes. You leave the loss on the field and get ready for the next game. It never rang more true for Cedartown as it did when it had to absorb the loss to LaFayette and get ready for the No. 5–rated Griffin Bears. The Bears came into the game loaded with talent and put on a clinic for passing and running the football as they crushed the 'Dogs 40–7.

But there was no time to sit around and lick their wounds because the next week was a big game at Barron Stadium against East Rome. Three times in the fourth quarter, Cedartown knocked on the door of the Gladiator goal line, and each time it was denied entrance when Wendell Rhodes's passes were intercepted near the goal line. In a game where Cedartown dominated in statistics and could have won, the Gladiators prevailed 19–14. Coach Carter said that his team was good enough to play with anyone when it executed on defense like it did on offense. He said that some players would have to play both ways until other players became good enough to play at their positions.

The Dalton Catamounts had not allowed a touchdown to be scored on them all season. A 0–0 tie to West Rome was their only blemish, and it looked like Bill Chappell's Cats were improving every game. Although the Cedartown Bulldogs averaged over 300 yards of offense every game, they were having problems crossing the goal line and were putting up just over 11 points a game. The Cedartown ground game was impressive, with Frank Burgess leading the way with 150 yards. Cedartown outgained Dalton 258 yards to 188 yards, but it was Dalton's passing game that carried the Catamounts as quarterback Mike Robinson completed seven of twelve passes for 136 yards and three touchdowns for a 34–6 Dalton victory. Now with a four-game losing streak, Coach Carter needed to reflect on how his team had gotten into this tailspin. He knew that they should have won the games against LaFayette and East Rome, which would have given them a 3-2 record with a winnable game coming up against Cass. A record of 4-2 with losses to Griffin and Dalton would be the making of a good season, but this is football, and a loss by 1 point is as bad as a loss by 40 points. From this point on, it had to be one game at a time.

A 20–6 win over Cass may have been just what the doctor ordered as Cedartown anticipated its match with defending state champion West Rome. Like Dalton, West Rome's defense was stingy, allowing only one touchdown all season. Senior tackles Anthony Slafta and Lane Brewer averaged over ten tackles a game and bolstered a defensive front that would be a tough test for hard-nosed fullback Burgess. Burgess was fifth in the region in rushing, gaining nearly 600 yards in six games. On the flip side, West Rome's Roger Weaver was the region's No. 1 ball carrier with 756 yards.

It was a tough, hard-hitting affair as Cedartown's defense rose to the occasion and played its best game of the year. Allowing West Rome only one touchdown and keeping the ball in Chieftain territory most of the night, the Bulldog defenders kept the game within reach until the fading minutes of the fourth quarter. A blocked punt set up West Rome's only score, and a missed extra point was the difference in the game as Cedartown went down 7–6 to West Rome. Burgess ran hard up the middle, gaining fifty-four yards. John Ayers ran for eighty yards and passed for fifty-five in another game that should have been a win for Cedartown. West Rome's coach, Paul Kennedy, said that Cedartown deserved a better fate for the game it had played.

In another game that was just above the horizon, Cedartown went down to Chattooga 14–6. In the last home game of the season, the 'Dogs beat Wills 39–6.

The 1966 team could go down as one of the great teams of Cedartown that just couldn't find the end zone. It had all the ingredients of a winning team. Its players could run and pass the football with the best in the region. When it was focused and ready to play, the defense was second to none. The team's only shortcoming was that sometimes it didn't score enough points, and that is what decides the outcome.

1967

Frank Burgess, Ty Johnson and Steve Russell were elected by the team to be captains for the 1967 season. Coach Carter liked the makeup and the intensity level the team brought to practice but had concerns about the overall team speed.

Making a second-half comeback attempt on the arm of Wendell Rhodes, the Bulldogs came up short, bowing to Cartersville 21–14. Rhodes completed twelve of seventeen passes for 140 yards and ran for 35 yards. Burgess picked up 65 yards on the ground.

Behind Frank Burgess's fifteen carries for seventy-five yards, Cedartown upended the Griffin Bears 7–6 in the second game of the season. Starting from the thirty-four-yard line, the 'Dogs used the remaining part of the first quarter and most of the second quarter to execute what would be the drive for the winning touchdown.

On the legs of Frank Burgess, the toe of Phillip Gammage and a determined defense, Cedartown edged the East Rome Gladiators 9–6. Burgess rushed for seventy-five yards, including a fourteen-yard run for the touchdown, but it was the defense that won the game for the Bulldogs. In the closing minutes of the game, East Rome marched to the Cedartown twenty-yard line, where the defense buckled down and stopped the Gladiators on downs. Moments later, Cedartown found its back up against the goal post when East Rome blocked a punt that rolled out of bounds at the fifteen-yard line. On the next play, Tommy Privett intercepted a pass that allowed Rhodes and company to run out the clock.

Cedartown's next task would be to visit the powerful Dalton Catamounts. The Cats had dropped their opener 7–6 to West Rome and had taken out their fury on any team that got in their path, including a 45–0 whipping of the 'Dogs.

Leaving the mess at Dalton in Dalton, the 'Dogs got back on the winning track with a 37–26 win against Cass. Frank Burgess exploded for 132 yards and two touchdowns on sixteen carries to lead all ball carriers. Tony Redding scored on an 80-yard kickoff return and 45-yard Wendell Rhodes pass as the Bulldogs remained in contention for the region title.

Winning the game in the statistical department and moving the ball inside West Rome's ten-yard line on three occasions, Cedartown let the game and perhaps the region championship slip away 14–7. Outgaining the Chieftains 266 yards to 159 yards and knocking at the door all night, the Bulldogs were only able to cash in for one score as the Chiefs took over first place. Burgess once again cracked the 100-yard barrier with 101 tough yards up the middle.

In a game marred by penalties and fisticuffs, the Chattooga Indians slipped into the Bulldog camp and rode away with a 14–13 victory on homecoming night, putting an end to any postseason hopes for Cedartown. Phillip Gammage connected on two field goal attempts but missed on two chances in the waning seconds of the game. Cedartown's defense held Chattooga to twenty-four yards rushing but was done in by a fumble that was returned to the Cedartown eight-yard line and a long touchdown pass that just got past the CHS defenders. Chattooga was flagged for a total of sixty yards in penalties to the Bulldogs' fifteen yards, but when Rhodes was injured and sidelined in the second quarter, the momentum of the game swung to the Indians.

The vaunted defense dominated the Rockmart Yellow Jackets in the annual cross-county rivalry, giving up only fifty-three yards as the 'Dogs prevailed 28–17. Coach Alton Gilmore lauded defensive ends Larry Davis and William Tanner for exceptional play.

In the final game of the year, Burgess rushed for a career-high 174 yards and Wendell Rhodes threw for 194 yards as Cedartown upset the LaFayette Ramblers 31–0. Noted for their play in this game were Tommy Beck, Jimmy Newsome and Denny Folsom.

CHAPTER 10

THE CEDAR HILL PANTHERS

O n the opposite side of town from Cedartown High School was Cedar Hill High School. Cedar Hill was the school for the black children from grades six through twelve. The Cedar Hill Panthers had a very successful high school football team that was coached by Escue Rodgers for the eighteen years that it existed. Cedar Hill had a record of 83-36-7, which is a winning percentage of .687. The Panthers won four state championships in the Georgia Interscholastic Association (GIA) and were perennially one of the best football teams in the state. Two of their championships were won on Gray Field in Cedartown. In 1964, the Panthers went 8-1-1 and were narrowly defeated 19–6 in their last game on Gray Field.

As far as high school records go, back to 1948 the Cedar Hill Panthers were a dominating football team. In their first season, they won five of seven games while playing most of them in Cedartown. In 1949, they won four games and lost one. Probably because of transportation problems, the Panthers had to forfeit four games that would have been played on the road in places like Collinsville, Alabama; Carrollton, Georgia; and even Atlanta.

Transportation loomed as a problem until about 1951, when they were able to play a full schedule of ten games, winning six, losing three and tying one. Standout players for the '51 team were Howard Colvin at halfback, Otis Cochran at fullback, Harold Orr at receiver and Eddie Bell at quarterback. After suffering two setbacks in the '51 season to LaFayette and Collinsville, Alabama, the Panthers inflicted some revenge by knocking off LaFayette 25–0 to win the North Georgia championship.

CHHS PANTHERS

Front Row: #26 Luther Gibson, #42 Tony Nelson, #41 Ed Bell, #47 Dexter Nelson, #25 Van Morgan, #33 Robert Jackson, #48 David Holiday, #27 Thomas Gibson , #29 Everett Willis, #30 Marion Brooks, #18 Ruben Chislom
Second Row: Head Coach; Mr. Escue Rodgers , #40 Ezzie Brown, #43 Freddie Malone, #31 Robert Lovelace, #28 Orange Green, #32 Alton Grant, #36 Otis Cothron, #44 Fred Barton, #45 Herman Reid, #39 Earnest Gibson, #34 Rayfus Smith, Mr. Odell Owens (Assistant Coach)

1953 STATE CHAMPS

MR. ESCUE RODGERS, HEAD COACH

The Cedar Hill High School Panthers. *Courtesy of Polk County Historical Society.*

Over one thousand fans braved temperatures below thirty degrees at Gray Field as the Cedar Hill Panthers defeated Dublin for the Class B state championship game. It had been a long climb to the top for Coach Rodgers and his Cats, but now that they were the champs, it was well worth the struggle.

Cedar Hill recovered a fumble on Dublin's first offensive play and moved the ball down to the goal line. Dublin's defense stiffened and stopped the Panthers on downs. Unable to move the ball, Dublin was forced to punt. Five plays later on first down, Colvin carried the ball in for the score. Before the first-quarter whistle had blown, Colvin broke free and galloped sixty yards to make the score 12–0. Late in the third quarter, Dublin climbed back into the game on a thirty-four-yard touchdown pass to make the score 12–6. The play that sealed the victory for Cedar Hill came after the Panthers' punt rolled dead at Dublin's one-yard line. On the next play, Dublin's quarterback went back to pass. Coming on a big inside rush, a defender blocked the pass that was caught on a shoestring catch by Cedar Hill's Eddie Hinkle, who didn't stop running until he was ten yards beyond the end zone.

1952

The excitement from 1951 spilled over into 1952 as the Panthers ran the table for a perfect 9-0 season, allowing only one touchdown to Collinsville, Alabama. New stars began to emerge in players like James Bell. In the game against Marietta, he carried the ball for over one hundred yards and returned two interceptions for over one hundred yards. Other newcomers were Fred Barton, Herman Reed and Dexter Nelson.

Repeating as North Georgia champions, the Panthers went down in defeat to a very good Tift County Industrial team in Tifton, 20–14.

1953

The loss at Tifton did nothing to quell the enthusiasm surrounding the Panthers, as Coach Rodgers had a record number of players report for the 1953 season. The squad was composed of six seniors: Ozzie Brown, tackle; Otis Cochran, halfback; Freddie Malone, tackle; Herman Reid, halfback; Ernest Gibson, end; and Charles Grant, guard. Surrounding this nucleus of veterans was an abundance of talent, including Dexter Nelson, fullback; Van Morgan, halfback; Rayfus Smith, guard; Robert Jackson, guard; Alton Grant and Marion Brooks, centers; Fred Barton, end; and Thomas Gibson and Ed Bell, two of the best quarterbacks in the state. Ed Bell was said to be the greatest athlete to ever play for Cedar Hill. The development players were Bobby Nelson, Edward Harris, Everett Willis, Robert Johnson, Luther Gibson and Tony Nelson.

These players blasted through their schedule with such focus and resolve that no team put up a serious threat throughout the season. When the fog had cleared and the final whistle had blown, the Cedar Hill Panthers sat on top of the football world with a perfect 10-0 season after walloping Jesup 74–13 to reclaim their crown as state champions.

The *Cedartown Standard* wrote, "The Cedar Hill Panthers soared to football fame this year mainly because of three factors—the sensational running of a 190 pound college bound halfback, the stout hearted tackling and blocking of several experienced boys, and the patient pounding of a one man coaching staff."

That halfback was Herman "Flash" Reid, and that coach was, of course, Escue Rodgers. After the game with Jesup, a coach from Atlanta's Morris Brown College offered scholarships to Reid, Fred Malone, Ozzie Brown and Otis Cochran. Fort Valley State and Florida's Bethune-Cookman University were also courting Reid.

1966–1968

Between 1966 and 1968, the Cedar Hill Panthers were dismantled as the players integrated with the Cedartown Bulldogs. Other history books carry pages of problems with integration in America. If they are to be truly representative, those pages will tell the story about how the black and white children in Cedartown generally got along very well. There were skirmishes and fisticuffs here and there, but black children and white children were not afraid to go to school every day because of constant racial tension. Bringing them into the Cedartown football program was the job of Ray Carter. This was simply another huge distraction to go along with replacing a legend. Ray stepped up and took on the task with a professional and no-nonsense approach when he laid down the rules that this was about winning football games, no matter what color a player's skin might be. The players from Cedar Hill made a slow transition from Panther to Bulldog. At the end of the 1967 season, Coach Carter saw another opportunity in the education field. He decided that he would rather be an administrator than a coach and took a job with the Polk County Board of Education.

With the proliferation of the Vietnam War and prospective football players choosing a more laid-back lifestyle over football, adding black players to a team that had an established system in place for its players as young as ten years old probably would require a great politician to be successful. That job would now belong to Bill Lundy.

CHAPTER 11

WELCOME TO CEDARTOWN, COACH LUNDY AND FAMILY

Bill Lundy is from Broken Bow, Oklahoma. He went to college at Northeastern State University in Oklahoma, where he lettered four years in football, two years in baseball and one year in basketball. In his senior year, he scored six touchdowns in one game and was selected to the all-conference team. He received his master's degree at Peabody College of Vanderbilt, where he met Coach French Johnson. When Johnson was hired to be head football coach and athletic director at Rockmart, he brought Lundy along to coach the offense. Lundy moved with Johnson to Marietta and was the offensive coordinator when the Blue Devils won the North Georgia championship and played for the state title.

He left Johnson to become head coach for Sandy Springs. In two years, he took Sandy Springs from being a team with a long history of losing to region champions. From there, he became principal and coach of College Park High School. One of the players at College Park was Bill Curry, who went on to play for Georgia Tech and the Baltimore Colts. It was through his College Park association with Marion Cumming that Coach Lundy was introduced to the Polk County School Board and offered the job of head coach and athletic director of Cedartown High School.

Coach Lundy is married to the former Betty June Smith of Rockmart, and they have three boys, Billy, Tony and Ricky, and one daughter, Kristie.

1968

Coach Lundy must have been thrilled when the 'Dogs went to Rockmart and shut out the Yellow Jackets on opening night 14–0. Cedar Hill transfer Demetrius Owens returned a kickoff for an eighty-five yard touchdown to seal the victory.

However, the very next week, Lundy discovered that being with Cedartown meant walking into every stadium with a big bull's-eye on your back, as Chamblee came to Cedartown and thumped the Bulldogs 21–3.

The next week, the Bulldogs got back into the win column with a win over Cartersville and began preparation for a battle with East Rome, with No. 2–ranked West Rome just around the bend.

Any of the fourteen men who had coached Cedartown in the sixty years of playing football would have agreed that at the beginning of a Cedartown career, a coach has to be ready and willing to take his knocks. Lloyd Gray took his, Shuler Antley took his, Doc Ayers took his and, more than likely, Bill Lundy was going to get some dings in his first year at the helm. It seemed to be part of the tradition.

On paper, East Rome looked like a team Cedartown could beat. The Gladiators were 1-2, with the only win being a 7–6 win over Model High School. It was unknown at the time that the one-touchdown loss to East Rome meant more than a region upset.

Lagging behind in the region standings, Cedartown fought a gallant fight, with the undefeated West Rome Chieftains losing by only a field goal. West Rome went on a three-game losing streak, including region losses to Cartersville and Pepperell. East Rome continued on its winning ways until it lost its annual rivalry match with West Rome. With only one loss in the region, East Rome was the 7AA South champion. The loss to East Rome is what cost the 'Dogs the sub-region championship. Five wins, five losses and being just one win from the region playoffs wasn't an unusual start for a coach just beginning his Cedartown career.

1969

Jimmy Carter returned to the fold at CHS when Bill Lundy hired him to coach defensive backs and offensive ends. The quarterback from the '63 state championship team was coming off a stellar career as a defensive back for the Auburn Tigers. Carter was drafted by the Pittsburgh Steelers but decided against playing pro football and returned to Cedartown.

There was a change in the extra point rules in 1969 that awarded a team two points for running or completing a pass across the goal line from the four-yard line instead of kicking the ball after it had been centered from the two-yard line to the holder. However, if the ball is snapped from the two-yard line to the kick holder, he is allowed to put the ball in play just as if he is a quarterback and make an attempt to fake the kick and run or pass it in for the two-point conversion.

Phillip Ferguson and Daniel Jackson were named captains of the 1969 version of the Bulldogs. Bruce Ware was named starting quarterback but was going to get a lot of pressure from Cedar Hill transfer Raymond Smith. Ware had been a starter since the eighth grade and had one year of experience with Lundy's playbook and cadence system. The old Doc Ayers way of calling signals departed with Ray Carter. Raymond Smith was fleet-footed and had a good throwing arm but was the new kid on the block, and beating out the reigning quarterback was going to take more than some flashy footwork.

Tough will and determination couldn't overcome serious offensive miscues as Rockmart cashed in two Cedartown turnovers to defeat the Bulldogs in front of a crowd of over seven thousand fans.

The next week's trip to Chamblee exposed serious defensive gaps in the secondary as the Bulldogs from DeKalb County scored on a sixty-four-yard pass and a forty-seven-yard pass in the first quarter. Outweighing the 'Dogs on the line of scrimmage by an average of twenty pounds a player, Chamblee shredded Cedartown's defense with long running plays and passed at will, opening up a 41–0 halftime lead. A Bruce Ware twenty-two-yard field goal in the third quarter was the only score for the Bulldogs.

After playing the East Rome Gladiators dead even through most of the game, Gladiator Robert Montgomery broke off big runs of fifty-four yards and seventy-seven yards to cave in the Bulldogs 20–7. Playing their best game of the year, the 'Dogs showed heart and determination in a game that was decided by two plays.

Coach Lundy decided to go with some of his younger players as he sent a message to his team and Bulldogs of the future that team rules were to be obeyed and breaking them had severe consequences. One newcomer to step into the spotlight was sophomore Allen Hunt. Hunt caught passes of thirty-two yards and grabbed a thirty-five-yard touchdown pass from Ware that knotted the game at 7–7 to end the first quarter. As inexperience leads to mistakes, West Rome cashed two Cedartown turnovers into touchdowns and defeated the 'Dogs 21–13.

A road loss to Cass, followed by losses to powerhouses Carrollton and North Springs, had the city and the team reeling at the possibility of losing every game of the season, a debacle that had never been witnessed in the history of Cedartown football.

The team fought on and continued to be competitive in every game. In the final game of the season, on a cold and snowy night as the clock wound down to zero, quarterback Raymond Smith gave the Bulldog faithful a glimpse of the future as he scrambled around in the backfield and finally broke free for a sixty-five-yard touchdown run that was called back on a penalty. On the subsequent play, Smith again scrambled around in the backfield and almost broke free. It was a tremendous display of heart and athleticism that has always been the mark of Cedartown football. That glimpse of the future was what the team would become when Cedar Hill High School and Cedartown High School became one.

1970

Cedartown students moved into a brand-new school that was built on a hill on the east side of town in 1970. Along with the ordinary high school, there was a vocational building and a greenhouse to make CHS the new Cedartown Comprehensive High School. Since the construction was not complete, the Bulldogs would continue to play at Gray Field until Cedartown Memorial Stadium was complete.

Coach Lundy prepared his squad of forty-one players knowing that a repeat of the '69 season would not be tolerated. The glow illuminating from the faces of Lundy and his assistants sent the message that they were anything but worried about this year's team. Coach Crook commented that it was the best group of linemen Cedartown had in quite a while. Seniors Roger Grant, Steve Sorrells, Joe McClendon, Bruce Vice and David Miller led the way over underclassmen Earl Davis, Tony Carter, Terry Ector, Larry Peek and Bob Worthington. Freshmen Lamar Looney, Lee Brown, Kim Roberts and Jim Baker were all pushing the older players as they prepared for the junior varsity season. Raymond Smith got the nod at quarterback, with Reuben Gibson at fullback, Allen Hunt at wingback and Gary Sherfield at tailback.

Raymond "The Rocket" Smith, "Rapid" Reuben Gibson and "Galloping" Gary Sherfield raced for 245 yards as Cedartown upended Darlington 31–7 to open the 1970 season. Smith was named Rome-area player of the week, and the *Rome News Tribune* named Coach Lundy coach of the week.

A forty-three-yard pass play set up the only score of the game as Rockmart defeated the Bulldogs 7–0. In a game that was dominated by great defensive play, Cedartown's most serious threat ended when Raymond Smith was pushed out of bounds at the twenty-yard line as the clock ran out.

Sparked by Raymond Smith's fifty-six-yard punt return for a touchdown, Cedartown came from behind to defeat No. 10 Troup County 26–14.

With the game on the line and less than four minutes to play, future NFL player Mike Hogan broke the hearts and crushed the hopes of the Cedartown faithful as he rambled sixty-six yards to give East Rome a 23–22 victory over the Bulldogs.

The dominating Cedartown defense held Cartersville to a field goal as the 'Dogs slipped away with a 6–0 win.

Set off by a barrage of twenty-two points in the second quarter, West Rome strolled to an easy 28–0 victory over Cedartown.

After a 6–0 win against Cass and a 46–8 blowout of Paulding County, the Bulldogs took aim at Pepperell. Using a ball control ground game, the Dragons dominated the clock in time of possession and yardage as they beat the 'Dogs 29–12.

With a record of five wins and four losses, Cedartown traveled to Murray County, wanting to end the season with a winning record. Missing Sherfield and Smith, Cedartown relied on Reuben Gibson, Everett Kelley and Donnie Lewis to lead the offense. Unable to move the ball, Cedartown was shut out until Frankie Woods blocked a punt and Steve Sorrells picked up the ball and ran in to score from the twenty-five-yard line. The Indians handed the Bulldogs a disappointing 14–8 loss and ended a season that had started out so full of hope.

Making the tough decision that the football team was not headed in the right direction, the board of education released Bill Lundy from his contract with the Cedartown Bulldogs. Lundy took over as principal of Model High School and later returned to Cedartown, where he continued his career as an educator and administrator. His three sons went on to become standout football players for CHS. His oldest son, Billy, and youngest son, Ricky, are now partners in a very successful law firm. They have the dubious distinction of trying a case before the U.S. Supreme Court and winning their case. Lundy's other son, Tony, is offensive coordinator for the Cedartown Bulldogs.

1971

Leaving a team he had coached for seventeen years and to two state championships, Jimmy Hightower was brought to Cedartown with the sole purpose of bringing the Bulldogs back to prominence in northwest Georgia.

Heading into the first game of the season, Hightower commented that the team was not ready to play. He was correct in his assessment, as Cedartown ran off four straight losses to begin the '71 season. It finally broke into the win column with a 12–0 win over Cartersville before taking a 29–0 trouncing by West Rome. The old coach had a little bit of time to work his plans, but a one-win and five-loss start had people up in arms about the direction he was taking the team. Sure, some of these teams were very good, but this was Cedartown, and the fans were not accustomed to losing to any of these teams that were now dominating the area.

Finally, with wins over Cass, Paulding County, Pepperell and Murray County, the 'Dogs ended the season on a four-game winning streak. With power runners Reuben Gibson and Michael Owens returning, the next year looked like the year Cedartown would return to the top of the region.

In 1971, Allen Hunt was named Mr. Bulldog. In 2002, Allen's son Sam was chosen Mr. Bulldog, and in 2007, Allen's son Van was chosen as Mr. Bulldog. It was a proud coronation for a family that includes Van Hunt, who played as a lineman on the 1937 team that didn't allow a point to be scored on it all season.

1972

If the '72 Bulldogs were going to turn things around and return to the top of the region, it would have to be without the services of Jimmy Hightower and most of his staff. The common belief is that LaGrange offered Hightower a lot of money to take the job as football coach and athletic director. After living in Cedartown less than one year, Hightower packed his bags and moved to LaGrange. Taking over the program with three years of coaching experience was former CHS quarterback Jimmy Carter. Carter was the players' choice, the fans' choice and the choice of the board of education. Coach Carter was an affable, handsome young man who never met a stranger. He had a great love for the students at Cedartown High, a great passion for the game of football and a loyalty to Cedartown that was immeasurable. The year before accepting the head coach position, Coach Carter had married the former Cedartown girls' basketball star Kathy Franklin, who was now a CHS teacher.

The season began with a lot of hope and high expectations. Putting together a three-game win streak at the beginning of the season had the team and the fans believing that better days had arrived. That all came to a screeching halt when the team turned in a lackluster performance in Rome's Barron Stadium and lost to Pepperell 7–6. Carter said he believed the team had lost its appetite for football and the players weren't hungry anymore.

That loss of appetite continued when the team traveled to play the Class A, No. 1–ranked Rockmart Yellow Jackets. Going the aerial route, Cedartown used passes from quarterback Chip Faires to Danny Kirby and Kim McClendon to set up Greg Wills's fifteen-yard run for a touchdown and a 7–0 lead. Rockmart answered with a long drive to even the score before halftime. Rockmart had a third-quarter punt return for a touchdown and put the game away on a long sixty-five-yard drive as the clock ticked away in the fourth. With three wins and two losses, the Bulldogs were in jeopardy of letting the season slip away as West Rome stood next in line.

In a game that was so reminiscent of the last few years, the West Rome Chieftains came to Gray Field and put a 34–7 drubbing on the Bulldogs.

Things improved with a 34–7 win over Cass, but East Rome was next on the schedule, and the Gladiators had only one loss on their record and were coming off a 51–0 trouncing of Pepperell. A bone-crushing 24–6 loss to East Rome put an end to any hopes of a special season.

1973

Hoping to build on a strong foundation, Coach Carter realized that he had a strong and athletic group of players returning for 1973. Senior running backs Charles West and Greg Wills were fast and had the power to break into the open field. Danny Kirby was a dependable wide receiver and was very elusive returning punts and kickoffs. Brad Goss and Chip Faires staged a heated battle for the quarterback position, with Goss getting the nod to begin the season as the starter. Lamar Daniel and Larry Peek anchored the line that was small but talented.

After Danny Kirby returned a punt to the Darlington twenty-nine-yard line, Charles West broke free for a touchdown to give the 'Dogs a 7–0 victory over Darlington. However, Brad Goss was injured and would be out for the season.

The Bulldogs held Sprayberry to three first downs and a total of sixty-six yards as Cedartown won the second game of the season 27–0.

On September 14, 1973, the Cedartown Bulldogs said goodbye to Gray Field and played the first game at Cedartown Memorial Stadium. As the Cedartown faithful christened a new stadium, the Chattooga Indians sent down a raiding party to remind the Bulldogs that football was war. The Indians took a few scalps and headed home with a 32–7 victory.

The Bulldogs appeared to be on the right track as they rambled for 138 yards in the first half against Pepperell. In spite of keeping the ball in Dragon territory most of the game, the 'Dogs only crossed the goal line once. Pepperell took advantage of a second-half turnover to salvage a 7–7 tie.

The next week, Rockmart's defense neutralized Cedartown's offense and capitalized on three fumbles to down the 'Dogs 34–0.

The 42–0 drubbing by West Rome ended Cedartown's chances at the playoffs but didn't kill the team's spirit. The boys jumped to their feet and beat Cass 25–13. After a hard-fought loss to East Rome, Cedartown ended the season with two decisive victories over Paulding County and Troup County.

1974

Running back Luther Pullen and quarterback Jeff Mullen led the way as Cedartown began 1974 with a 27–0 shutout of Calhoun.

Chattooga defeated the 'Dogs 13–0 even though they gave up 105 yards in penalties. The Bulldogs came back the next week to defeat LaFayette 42–0, but back-to-back losses to Rockmart and West Rome took them out of contention for the region championship. The final record of four wins and six losses had fans beginning to wonder if Cedartown's football tradition had reached the end of the trail.

1975

After a 6–6 tie with Pepperell, the 'Dogs looked forward to the meeting with Chattooga. In the previous encounter, the Indians had shown a little too much enthusiasm as they ran up the score on Cedartown. Sparked by Billy Lundy's fifty-yard pass to Joe Davis, the 'Dogs jumped to an early lead. The defending 6AA champions thwarted several Cedartown drives and displayed some firepower of their own to win 20–6.

In a comeback 20–7 win against LaFayette, sophomore Joe Davis began to reveal himself as a serious athlete. He was catching passes from Lundy and running for huge chunks of yardage off tackle or on end sweeps. Another sophomore, Randy Cook, was making himself a home in the backfield as a tough inside runner and a punishing blocker. From the linebacker position, Cook had an uncanny ability to read defenses and meet runners at the line of scrimmage.

The Bulldogs battled Rockmart to a scoreless tie for three quarters, but the Yellow Jackets scored in the fourth quarter to win 7–0.

Facing an undefeated West Rome team, the boys from Cedartown showed new life when Billy Lundy threw a twenty-nine-yard touchdown pass to Mike Wilson for a 7–0 lead in the fourth quarter. The Chieftains managed a late touchdown to tie, but for the first time in a few years, Cedartown was in playoff contention.

James Moore picked up a fumble and ran sixty-eight yards for a touchdown, intercepted three passes and blocked a punt to lead Cedartown to a 14–6 win over Cass.

The 'Dogs were not able to overcome three turnovers against East Rome's talented defense and fell 12–0.

Coosa unveiled a new passing attack to aid its dominant running game and handily defeated the 'Dogs 26–13.

Cedartown went on to win the last two games and finish the season at 4-4-2. Not quite a winning season, but this team showed flashes of brilliance that left hope for the future.

With players like Lundy, Cook and Davis returning and some bright prospects in the junior high, Coach Carter had reasons to be optimistic. Unfortunately, someone knew of a coach in South Georgia who was a sure bet to turn around the Cedartown football team. Obviously someone had enough authority or enough influence to make the change of head coach at Cedartown High School. Like the high-class man of integrity he is, Jimmy Carter relinquished his role as head football coach and became an administrator, high school principal and superintendent of Polk County schools.

CHAPTER 12

THE WINDS OF CHANGE

1976

With gale-force winds gusting to over forty miles an hour, the Cedartown Bulldogs splashed through buckets of mud, slammed an old rival and served notice to region 7AA and the state of Georgia that the "old Dog" from Cedartown wasn't dead; he was merely sleeping. With a new coach, a gun-slinging quarterback and a bunch of Cedartown boys who were hungry to win, the mighty canine from northwest Georgia raised his head, looked out of his house and came onto a brand-new field with a brand-new style of football.

When quarterback/kicker Ted Peeples put his toe on the leather to start the 1976 season, it was the beginning of a transformation that took the Cedartown Bulldogs from the doormat of high school football back to its rightful place at the top of the region standings. The Bulldogs had a seven-game losing streak going against their nastiest rival, the cross-county Rockmart Yellow Jackets. It could not have come at a better time or against a better opponent if it had been scripted in Hollywood.

Rockmart won the coin toss and decided to receive the kickoff. The Bulldogs elected to defend the goal with the wind to their backs. Peeples's kick, aided by the wind, sailed through the end zone. On fourth down, Rockmart had to punt into a wind that was so strong that folding chairs blew off the press box. The snap from center got away from the Rockmart punter, and Cedartown recovered on the ten-yard line. Two plays later, Joe Davis broke through over the right side for the score.

Coach Hill with the "Voice of the Bulldogs," WGAA radio announcer Frank Burgess. *Courtesy of John Hill.*

Once again, Peeples's kick sailed through the end zone and gave Rockmart the ball on its twenty-yard line. The Yellow Jackets moved the ball eighteen yards but were forced to punt into the wind. The punt garnered fourteen yards and put Cedartown in business inside the fifty-yard line. After an exchange of penalties, Davis took the ball for the second time of the night and raced fifty-one yards for the score.

For the third time, Peeples kicked through the end zone and Rockmart started on the 20-yard line. This time, instead of punting on fourth down, Rockmart coaches went for a first down. Cedartown stopped the quarterback sneak in its tracks and took over deep in Rockmart territory. One pass from Peeples to Billy Lundy and two runs by Davis put Cedartown up 20–0 with thirty-four seconds remaining in the first quarter. By the time it was over, Davis had rushed for 151 yards and Chuck Knowles for another 90 as John Hill picked up his first win as Cedartown coach.

Coach Hill played his high school football in Pompano Beach, Florida. His road to Cedartown came directly through Camden County, Georgia, where he had a five-year record of 40-11-1. In his last season, his Wildcats ran off a string of 11 straight victories before they were defeated by Americus in the state quarterfinals. Now he was in Cedartown, a small town with a big football tradition. Even as a boy growing up in Florida, he had heard of Cedartown's many trips to play Bay County High. Perhaps wanting to be part of that rich tradition was one of the many reasons Hill came to Cedartown.

From the first game, Cedartown put together a five-game winning streak before meeting the always-dangerous West Rome Chieftains. West Rome was having a less-than-average year and had won only two games and lost three going into the Cedartown game. The way Peeples was bombarding the air with long passes and Davis was breaking away with long runs, everyone believed that Cedartown would handle the Chieftains with little problems— everyone except West Rome. Cedartown was never able to control the momentum of the game and left the door open just enough for Bobby Bowling to break away on a ninety-seven-yard run and steal the victory for West Rome. Some people brushed it off as a letdown from the big game on the road against an undefeated Walhalla, South Carolina team that had thrown the 'Dogs' momentum off. After putting together another five-game winning streak, Cedartown carried its 10-1 record to Rome to decide who was going to be the region champion.

Before a crowd of six thousand, West Rome took the opening kickoff, ran two plays and fumbled the ball away to Cedartown. On the first play from scrimmage, Peeples hit Daryl Prior in the end zone to put the 'Dogs up 7–0. West Rome answered on a long, time-consuming drive that featured quarterback Johnny Tutt running the option play to perfection. Tutt himself picked up nice gains, but the big play came on a pitch to Bowling that netted twenty-five yards. Tutt dropped back and passed twelve yards to Tim Roberson to make the score 7–7. With one minute and forty-eight seconds left in the first half, Tutt fumbled, and Cedartown recovered on West Rome's forty-eight-yard line. Aided by a pass interference call against West Rome, Peeples lofted a pass to the end zone that James Chandler battled to catch, and Cedartown was on top at intermission 14–7.

Cedartown received the second-half kickoff and moved the ball to the West Rome thirty-two-yard line before West Rome stopped Davis on fourth down. Pulling out the trick playbook, West Rome caught Cedartown's defensive backs out of position and completed a halfback pass down to the ten-yard line. From there, Cedartown held and West Rome kicked a field goal to make the game closer at 14–10. Cedartown punted the ball to the Chieftains' twenty-four-yard line with nine minutes to play. West Rome used a mix of running plays to get the ball to the Cedartown thirty-two-yard line. It seemed like the drive had stalled when West Rome was faced with fourth down and needed six yards to make a first down. Tutt scrambled around in the backfield and threw the ball into the end zone. Andrew Oldham stretched out and caught the ball in the corner to put the Chieftains in front 17–14.

With plenty of time left on the clock, the 'Dogs took over at the twenty-yard line, but on the first play, quarterback Peeples fumbled the snap, giving West Rome the ball and the victory 17–14. It was a disappointing end to a great season, but it was a season that brought back the hope and enthusiasm about Cedartown football.

Ted Peeples was named to the *Atlanta Journal-Constitution* all-state team. He was given a scholarship to play football for Georgia Tech, where he was an outstanding punter.

1977

The new season brought some changes to the Bulldogs' lineup. Gone were Ted Peeples, Joe Davis, Billy Lundy and other stars from the '76 team. Returning were linebackers Randy Cook and Tim Mull, defensive back Mike C. Hill, running backs Daryl Prior and Larry Chubb and linemen Rory Gibson, Tim Mosely and Brad Paris. Altogether, Coach Hill dressed out over fifty players on the Cedartown sideline.

Taking over at quarterback was senior Ned Elrod. What Elrod lacked in game experience, he made up for with football savvy and a will to win football games. He was thin at five feet, nine inches and wasn't tall enough to be a prototype quarterback, but if he had been in John Hill's offensive system a couple more years, there would have been a number of colleges wanting to talk to him.

The nucleus of this team was solid, and there was enough muscle along the offensive line to open holes for Chubb and Prior. The defense was strong and capable of shutting down any offense in the area.

Things started out a little bit shaky. After an easy win over Rockmart, a 0–0 tie with Chattooga County had a lot of people wondering if this turnaround was real or if the addition of Ted Peeples had the bunch from Cedartown playing at an unusually high level. After shutting out Paulding County, Coosa, Rockmart and Walhalla, the trip up to Barron Stadium in Rome to play the West Rome Chieftains would determine if the Bulldogs were contenders or pretenders. Although West Rome's record of 2-1-2 didn't look too threatening, the Chieftains could always be counted on to play tough against the Bulldogs.

Avoiding disaster all night, Cedartown relied on great defensive plays to hold the game to a 0–0 tie. Rory Gibson and Dwayne Puckett each had big defensive stops. As the 'Dogs were backed into the wall, Mike C. Hill intercepted a West Rome pass at the Cedartown thirteen-yard line.

From there, Cedartown got back on track, reeling off four more victories until it caught a muddy field in Bowdon. The Red Devils made no secret of the fact that they were out to avenge their only loss from the year before at the hands of the Bulldogs. The 'Dogs got on the scoreboard first when Ned Elrod hit Daryl Prior for a forty-three-yard touchdown pass. Larry Chubb's kick for the extra point failed, and Cedartown led 6–0. On its next possession, Cedartown drove to the Bowdon seventeen-yard line before giving it up on downs. It was the last time the Bulldogs would approach the Bowdon goal line until late in the fourth quarter. Bowdon used up most of the third quarter to drive the length of the field for a touchdown and conversion that put them ahead 7–6. With the clock winding down, Cedartown drove from its twenty-one-yard line to the Bowdon twenty-yard line, but a penalty moved it back to the thirty-five-yard line, where Chubb missed a thirty-five-yard field goal as the clock wound down to zero.

1978 player Randy Cook. *Courtesy of Mrs. Jeanene Cook Austin.*

Cedartown's record of 7-1-2 was good enough to give the Bulldogs the 7AA South championship and the right to play West Rome for the region championship. Things looked bad for Cedartown when West Rome scored a quick touchdown to start the game and got worse when Elrod fumbled the snap, giving the Chieftains the ball deep at midfield. Two plays later, Randy Cook fell on a West Rome fumble that breathed new life into a Bulldog team that was in need of a break. Runs by Chubb and Elrod moved the ball down to the ten-yard line, and John Johnson bulled it over from there. Starting at the thirty-yard line, the 'Dogs used fourteen plays to take it into the end zone and led 13–7 at halftime. As Cedartown's defense slammed the door on West Rome, the offense continued to make long, methodical drives down the field as the Bulldogs handled the Chieftains 31–7. At the final horn, the Cedartown Bulldogs were once again champions of 7AA.

For the first time in the history of Cedartown Memorial Stadium, there would be a playoff game, as the Gordon Generals from Atlanta faced the 7AA champions. It was a game of offensive fireworks on one side and workhorse determination on the other. Taking the first quarter to shake off the excitement and nervous energy, Gordon capped a long drive with a twenty-yard touchdown pass to take the lead at 7–0. Cedartown answered by driving the ball seventy-one yards, with Larry Chubb taking it into the end zone from nine yards out to tie the score. Gordon wasted no time and retaliated with a seventy-eight-yard march, but the try for a 2-point conversion was stopped by Cedartown to hold the lead at 13–7.

Cedartown took the second-half kickoff and drove the ball seventy-four yards in thirteen plays. Ned Elrod flipped to John Johnson on a version of the shoestring play to convert the 2-point attempt, and Cedartown went ahead 15–13. Again, Gordon answered by covering sixty-four yards in eight plays for a touchdown. They missed the 2-point attempt but were back on top 19–15.

Starting at the sixteen-yard line, Cedartown drove eighty-four yards on a seventeen-play drive that ended with John Johnson going in from the three-yard line. Unfortunately, the six minutes and twenty-four seconds remaining was plenty of time for the Generals to regroup their offense and make one last drive that put them ahead to stay as Cedartown was left with only a few seconds to run three plays. In a great football game that could have gone either way, Cedartown ended its season with a 27–21 loss.

1978

Cedartown opened the 1978 season ranked No. 1 in the state by the *Atlanta Journal and Constitution*. Finding teams to play suddenly became difficult as John Hill looked toward Atlanta and teams in higher classifications. Gone were Chattooga, Bowdon and Haralson County as McEachern, Sprayberry and Douglas County stepped in to take on the mighty Bulldogs.

Not much changed in player personnel as players like Fred Berkeley, Dwayne Puckett, Rory Gibson, Randy Cook, Larry Chubb and Daryl Prior reported to camp bigger, stronger and faster. In the case of Puckett, it was bigger, as the offensive tackle weighed in at over 300 pounds. Lining him up next to 280-pound Wallace Jones gave the Cedartown Bulldogs the biggest offensive line in the state of Georgia, including the Atlanta Falcons, the Georgia Bulldogs and the Georgia Tech Yellow Jackets.

As the defense dominated the opponents and the offense—now led at quarterback by Daryl Prior—shredded opposing defenses, Cedartown won the first two games. A lackluster tie with Sprayberry and a close win over Coosa convinced the pollsters that the 'Dogs were not No. 1 quality, and they dropped them down to as far as No. 8.

Even though Paulding County played to within a field goal of upsetting Cedartown, the Bulldogs had become a well-oiled machine that won the sub-region and region championships.

For the second year in a row, the 'Dogs were headed to state competition as the Dalton Catamounts waited for a visit from an old rival. Cedartown hadn't beaten Dalton since 1963 and had been shut out by the Cats the last two times they played.

Dalton took an early 7–0 lead, and from that point on, Dalton's punter, Jimmy Arnold, pinned Cedartown in a hole for most of the game. Arnold's forty-four-yard average says nothing about the bad field position Cedartown had to begin its offense. His shortest punt of thirty-three yards rolled dead at the Cedartown seven-yard line. Not being able to stage an offensive threat, Cedartown's defense kept it close until a fourth-quarter punt of twenty-two yards rolled out of bounds at the Cedartown twenty-eight-yard line. With five minutes and four seconds remaining in the game, Dalton's Kenny Sharp found Bill Joyner in the corner of the end zone for a fifteen-yard touchdown. After Cedartown was stopped on fourth down at the thirty-yard line, Dalton had no problems putting the game away 20–0.

Dwayne Puckett, Daryl Prior and Wallace Jones were named to the *Atlanta Journal-Constitution* all-state team. Jones and Puckett were given scholarships to play football for the University of Georgia.

1979

By running off five wins in a row, it looked like the Cedartown Bulldogs had simply reloaded their roster, but suddenly some new foes entered the scene by way of Carrollton and Cass. An unexpected loss to the Trojans was an eye-opener, but losing to the Cass Colonels, who had only one win all season, had the Bulldogs reeling. When Rockmart joined the fracas and beat the 'Dogs 13–0, Coach Hill suddenly found his 'Dogs on a three-game losing streak.

Calling on veterans like David Wheeler, Tim Mull and Todd Mayben to lead the way along the line of scrimmage and Fred Berkeley, Lamar Whatley and Ricky Lundy to provide an offensive spark, the 'Dogs responded with wins over Paulding County and McEachern to set the ship back on course.

When the dust had settled, the new region format put the Bulldogs on the road against Carrollton for the first round of the playoffs. In a game played in a torrential downpour, it came down to a 0–0 tie, with the outcome determined by Cedartown penetrating to the Trojan seven-yard line while holding Carrollton at its own forty-four-yard line, giving Cedartown a 1–0 win.

In a game marred by turnovers, Rockmart gave Cedartown a taste of its own medicine by taking a 1–0 overtime win that was based on penetration. Cedartown and Rockmart each had three passes intercepted and lost three fumbles in a game that looked like no one wanted to win. In a wild and furious season, Cedartown settled for region runner-up with eight wins and four losses.

1980

In 1980, Cedartown began the season with a lot of momentum and didn't face a hurdle until the tenth game of the season, when the offense went cold. Not taking advantage of four scoring opportunities, the 'Dogs fell to the Carrollton Trojans 7–0. The 9-1 season record was good enough to give them home field advantage in the first round against Rossville. The blue Bulldogs from the north had learned their lesson from the 30–0 drubbing Cedartown had put on them two weeks earlier and played the Bulldogs close but eventually caved in to lose 14–0.

The Chattooga Indians came to Cedartown with every intention of pulling off the upset as they played Cedartown even, with the difference in the game being a missed extra point. It would be Cedartown to travel to Gwinnett County and play the undefeated Black Knights.

In Cedartown's poorest showing of the year, it gained only sixty-five yards on offense, made only four first downs and turned the ball over three times as the Black Knights defended their territory and chased the 'Dogs back home by a score of 34–0.

Verdis Boone was named to the *Atlanta Journal-Constitution* all-state team.

1981

One of the most talented offensive backfields in the history of Cedartown assembled to defend the previous year's championship. Junior Jeff Burger returned at quarterback, Clarence Calhoun and Reggie Whatley at halfback and David Barrow at fullback. Whatley had rushed for over one thousand yards in the previous season, while Calhoun was close behind with over seven hundred yards. Barrow was the workhorse, getting his yardage in the middle of the line. Burger won the quarterback job as a freshman and had shown steady improvement each year.

Having to replace every player on the offensive line of scrimmage was the key to the success of the 'Dogs. Coach Hill tagged Timmy Little at center, Joe Doyle Lanham and Steve Rush at tackles, Mike Casey and Jerry Ammons at the guard positions, Randy Surrett and Rodney Ellison at tight end and Ricky Hulsey at split end. On the defensive side, Hill boasted that he had the best group of linebackers since he had arrived in Cedartown in Randy Surrett, Steve Floyd and all-state prospect Verdis Boone. The inside defensive linemen were Rush, Lanham, Jeff Clay and David Duggan. Olin Gammage, Benny Landrum, Jeff Ruark and Jeff Couch would handle the defensive end positions. Richard Beavers, Ronny Irby or Rudy Diamond would play the cornerback position, and Vincent Sherfield would play safety.

In the first game against Lithia Springs, Cedartown had 409 yards of offense. Clarence Calhoun rushed for 151 yards. By the eighth game, Calhoun and David Barrow had amassed over 1,000 yards. The Bulldog team had become a machine that ran over anything in its path—until the Coosa Eagles came for a homecoming visit. Playing like a team of inexperienced sophomores, the 'Dogs committed too many turnovers to a team that was fired up and convinced it could win. With the game knotted at 14, Ruark picked up a fumble and raced 65 yards to put Cedartown in front 20–14 to stay.

The next week, Doc Ayers had to be smiling when he looked in the newspaper and saw that Cedartown had taken Rossville to the wood shed and gave them a good whipping to the score of 45–8.

Winning a tough game against an always-tough Carrollton made the Cedartown Bulldogs the undefeated and untied 7AAA South champions. When the 'Dogs put away Northwest Whitfield, the stage was set for another bout with longtime rival Dalton. One of the most successful teams to ever don the red and black had one serious flaw of fumbling the football. The team that scored more points than any team in Bulldog history gave away any chance of winning the elusive state championship when it turned the ball over to Dalton five times on fumbles. It looked like Cedartown had gained some momentum when Jeff Burger went over from the one-yard line. Leading 20–14, Dalton's sure-handed quarterback, Preston Poage, engineered a sixteen-play drive that ran the clock down to zero and made Dalton the 7AAA champions.

Verdis Boone was named to the *Atlanta Journal-Constitution* all-state team for the second straight year.

1982

With a boatload of lettermen returning, John Hill's Bulldogs began the 1982 season ranked No. 2 in the state behind Bainbridge. Lurking in the shadows and ranked No. 4 were the Dalton Catamounts. When the No. 9–ranked Marist War Eagles came to Cedartown on opening night, the ole 'Dog marked every corner of the end zone, cornered that bird and wrung its neck by a score of 61–28. The next poll established Cedartown at No. 1. In what was becoming the usual manner, the Cedartown first string played for the first half and let the substitutes play the second, as they became the first Cedartown team to have back-to-back undefeated regular seasons. They scored more points than the '81 team and used their second string in every game.

Stumbling only to powerhouse West Rome, Dalton had secured enough wins to gain home field advantage in the region championship game. There were a lot of questions that this veteran team of Bulldogs had to answer if they wanted to get past a nasty cat and advance to the state finals, and first on the list was: can they hold on to the football?

On a rain-soaked field, Cedartown's Jeff Burger hit Reggie Whatley for a thirty-three-yard touchdown pass on the opening drive of the game, and everyone knew that Cedartown had come to play. Dalton answered by driving the ball eighty yards in ten plays. The missed extra point kept the Bulldogs in the lead 7–6. Cedartown was flagged for a penalty on fourth and one and had to punt. Dalton went seventy-five yards in twelve plays to take the lead 14–7 after the 2-point conversion attempt was good.

Holding that lead until the third quarter, Dalton scored again when Ricky Farmer intercepted a Jeff Burger pass and ran sixty yards for the score. The missed extra point gave the Catamounts a 20–7 lead. The teams began the fourth quarter in a driving rain, making it difficult to move the football down field. When Dalton's punter, Allen McGill, mishandled the snap, Cedartown recovered on the seven-yard line. Burger carried it in to score, and the score was Dalton 20 and Cedartown 14. As Dalton was running out the clock, the ball popped loose, and Cedartown recovered on the forty-three to have one last chance with forty-eight seconds left. Two Burger passes took the ball to the twenty-eight-yard line. On Burger's third attempt, McGill stepped in front of wide receiver Richard Beavers for the interception and ended Cedartown's perfect season by the same score as the year before, 20–14.

Jeff Burger and Dennis Buffington were named to the *Atlanta Journal-Constitution* all-state team. Jeff Burger received a scholarship to play football for the University of Auburn, where he played quarterback. After his senior season with Auburn, Jeff was named all-SEC quarterback.

1983

With the remaining static electricity generated by the previous two years of dominating football, Coach Hill hoped to spring off that momentum into a rebuilding year and return to the top of the region standings.

Van Dingler got the nod to replace all-star Jeff Burger and lead an inexperienced but exuberant group of about sixty players who, like their predecessors, were hungry for a championship team. Dexter Montgomery, Tony Davis and Allen Price rounded out a backfield that followed veteran linemen Dennis Buffington, Darron Evans and Jimmy Chaflin. Sophomores Joey Rice and Eric Collins added depth to the offensive line. Rice, Collins, Evans and Buffington joined Kermit Whatley, Scott Temple, Ronnie Irby, Mike Munford, Allen Garrett and Frank Jackson to make up the core of a defense that Coach Hill hoped would be ready to jell by the time Cedartown began region play against Coosa.

As expected, the trip to Marist in Atlanta exposed Cedartown's need for work on defense as Marist came away with a 28–16 win.

Holding Anniston to one touchdown and Rockmart to only a field goal gave the team momentum going into region play. The 'Dogs downed Coosa and Pepperell on back-to-back Friday nights but were caught off guard by an upstart team from Cass. The Colonels came to town with a vaunted defense and an undefeated record. In a game that went down to the wire and ultimately decided the region championship, Cass slipped away with a

14–7 victory. Although the 'Dogs kept up the good fight, Cass was not to be undone as they ran the table in for the sub-region title and beat Carrollton to be crowned region champions.

1984

Although a 7-3 record to end the '83 season was respectable, it was less than acceptable coming out of the Jeff Burger years. Although Burger was phenomenal, Hill and the rest of the Cedartown faithful had become accustomed to rolling over area opponents with ease and having a place in the region and state playoffs. 1984 saw the return of an old opponent from the lower AA classification that was rolling over every team in its path and had been for more than two years. The West Rome Chieftains entered the season with a thirty-four - (yes, thirty-four) game winning streak. By the fourth game of the season, that streak had hit thirty-eight as Hill's Bulldogs strapped on their gear to try to slay the mighty giant.

Cedartown used a combination of tenacious defense and great punts by Buzz Payne to keep the Chiefs pinned down deep in their own territory. Little by little, West Rome gained field advantage. As the clock wound down before halftime, West Rome had advanced to Cedartown's eleven-yard-line. The 'Dogs defense stiffened, and the Chiefs settled for a field goal attempt that went wide to go into the locker room tied at 0–0.

Cedartown returned the second-half kickoff to its twenty-two-yard line. After three negative plays, Payne punted from the Cedartown end zone. West Rome was in business at Cedartown's forty-two-yard line, and the field position was now in its favor. On the third play from scrimmage, Ralph Johnson burst through over left tackle and sprinted thirty-five yards to break the deadlock and put West Rome on the scoreboard.

Cedartown's Jimmy Lemeka returned the kickoff to the Cedartown thirty-one, but on the next play, the 'Dogs fumbled and West Rome recovered. Three plays later and another extra point put the Chieftains up 14–0. Not being able to muster much offense, the Bulldogs caught a break when James Atkins recovered a fumble at West Rome's thirty-four-yard line. On the first play of the fourth quarter, Kermit Whatley dove over the goal line for a Cedartown touchdown. An attempt for a 2-point conversion failed, and Cedartown trailed 14–6. Cedartown's defense came to life and stopped West Rome on downs. The 'Dogs began to move the football until a fifteen-yard penalty killed the momentum, forcing the Bulldogs to punt. The Chiefs used up most of the fourth quarter driving the ball down field and scoring the touchdown that put the game out of reach.

In football, the two biggest side affects of a big game are the game before and the game after the big game. Teams sometimes look ahead to that big game and don't prepare for the opponent they are about to play. Often, teams suffer a letdown on the following game, particularly if they lose the big game. Perhaps Anniston was the better team or Cedartown suffered a letdown coming out of the West Rome game, but the final results of the 17–13 loss left Cedartown with two straight losses heading into region play.

Showing the grit of a champion, Cedartown put together a six-game winning streak that gave it the sub-region championship and a match with Murray County for the region title. The 'Dogs had an 11–0 lead and seemed to be in control of the game until late in the second quarter, when a clipping penalty forced them to punt from near their own end zone. A short punt gave Murray County its best field position of the night. A questionable pass interference call on fourth down gave the Indians another set of downs and energized their offense. On fourth and six from the fourteen-yard line, Indian quarterback Patrick Baynes tossed a pass to Roger Rainey to put the Indians on the board as the first half ended.

In the second half, the Bulldogs pounded the ball at the Murray County offense. They moved the chains down the field, but a tough, hard-hitting Indians defense either stopped the 'Dogs or created a turnover. With the score Cedartown 11 and Murray County 6, Baynes unloaded a seventy-four-yard touchdown bomb to Rainey that stunned Cedartown and had Murray County rocking the bleachers.

The Bulldogs did not quit as they drove the ball to the Murray County ten-yard line. On fourth down, John Barrow's field goal sailed wide of the goal posts. Five plays later, Baynes hit Keith Swilling with a fifty-two-yard touchdown pass that sealed the victory for the Indians. Cedartown had controlled the football and the line of scrimmage for most of the game, but two big plays by a quarterback with a big arm were the difference in the game.

1985

With a team of hard-nosed seniors returning, John Hill believed the '85 team to be full of promise. Usual foes like Dalton and Carrollton stood in the doorway to the region title. There was this huge problem coming down from Rome in the name of the West Rome Chieftains, who didn't matter as far as the region or the state playoffs were concerned, but no team worthy of the title "Champion" could stand to lose to anyone on its home turf.

After an easy win over Ringgold, the 'Dogs fell into a losing streak that threatened to put a damper on the season before region play commenced. An unlikely loss to Rockmart set the Bulldogs on their heels, and although a 24–8 loss to Dalton didn't knock them out, the 49–0 roundhouse from West Rome had everyone ready to throw in the towel on 1985.

The fans and coaches began to feel better when the Bulldogs shut out Anniston 36–0, but the team came together and returned to reality when a tough Calhoun team played it tooth and nail in a hard-hitting football game. Calhoun running back Amos Washington pounded the Cedartown line and tore off chunks of yardage, amassing 205 yards on twenty-six carries. Believing Cedartown was having a down year, the Yellow Jackets made a statement that they were in this region to win. Cedartown answered back that it was the king of the hill and intended to stay on top. Calhoun's attempt for a 2-point conversion fell short as the Bulldogs triumphed 28–26 and set out to take on the rest of region 7AAA.

After a 20–19 nail-biting victory over Carrollton, Cedartown traveled to LaFayette and barely came away with the win. The Ramblers played them to a 7–7 tie at the end of regulation play, but the Bulldogs came through in overtime to take the 13–7 victory.

A 40–7 win over Cass set up the sub-region showdown with Southeast Whitfield. Playing its best game of the year, Cedartown handled the Raiders 41–20 to set up another match with Dalton.

Trailing 8–0 at halftime, an injured Van Dingler returned to lead the Bulldogs to a 20–8 victory over Dalton and make the Cedartown Bulldogs the 1985 7AAA champions. Dingler passed for 154 yards as Cedartown played error-free football while capitalizing on five Dalton turnovers. Back in September, no one would have believed that the 'Dogs would have gotten off the mat and climbed the big hill to the top.

The Bulldogs went on the road to Atlanta's Lakewood Stadium to take on the Walter F. George Falcons. In a driving rain that came down for the entire game, Cedartown shut down the George offense and turned a fumble into points as it won the quarterfinal round of the state playoffs and brought the semifinal and North Georgia championship game to Cedartown. Allen Lee was the hero when he picked up a fumble and rambled down the sideline untouched for a fifty-four-yard touchdown run.

Gainesville brought in a Red Elephant squad that had only been beaten once and had given up more than one touchdown only once all season. In the second quarter, Cedartown used a balanced attack to drive the ball from their thirty-eight-yard line to pay dirt. The key plays on the drive were a twenty-two-yard pass from Dingler to Payne on third down and Allen Price running up the middle for sixteen yards to the Red Elephant two-yard line. Lawayne Ridgeway scored from there to put the 'Dogs ahead 7–0.

Cedartown's offense continued to knock on the door, but penalties and the tough Gainesville defense kept the 'Dogs out of scoring position. Meanwhile, the Cedartown defense continued to keep Gainesville at bay until the five-minute mark of the fourth quarter, when the Elephants had a first down on the Bulldog twelve-yard line. The stadium rocked as the home team chanted loudly "DEFENSE! DEFENSE!" On the first play, the runner was stuffed for no gain. Once again, the Red Elephants tried the heart of the Cedartown defense, but it did not budge. On third down, a slant to the tail back picked up zero yardage. After a fourth-down snuff, the Bulldogs took possession of the ball still sitting on the twelve.

Cedartown ran three plays and punted. Gainesville took over the ball at its forty-seven-yard line with three minutes and fifty-seven seconds left in the ballgame. Seven plays later, it faced a fourth and two at the Cedartown seven-yard line with one minute and eleven seconds to go. Once again, the fans rose to their feet and chanted "DEFENSE! DEFENSE!" Cedartown's defense pushed back the Red Elephant linemen and tackled Gainesville's fullback for a two-yard loss. Cedartown Memorial Stadium exploded with excitement. The Cedartown Bulldogs were the North Georgia AAA champions and were going to play Thomson for the state championship. It had been twenty-two years since the mighty Bulldogs had played for the title of state champion.

The Thomson Bulldogs, coached by the great Luther Welsh, were the defending AAA champions. The only blemish on their record in Welsh's two-year tenure was a 14–14 tie with Newton County. Thomson's tradition went back nearly as far as Cedartown's, as it boasted three state championships.

The game started out as a defensive struggle until the second quarter, when Thomson's Craig Reece broke off a fifty-yard run that put the Thomson Bulldogs deep into Cedartown territory. Three plays later, the Thomson quarterback sneaked in for a touchdown to put Thomson ahead. The kick for the extra point failed, and the score was 6–0 in favor of the home team.

Thomson seemed to be taking control of the game as it drove seventy-one yards to take a 13–0 lead. Cedartown was still unable to move the football and punted. On the first play from scrimmage, Allen Lee picked up a Thomson fumble and ran forty-five yards for a touchdown that pulled Cedartown to within six points. Before the crowd could measure the momentum, Thomson's Andrew Williams took the kickoff straight up the middle for a ninety-nine-yard touchdown that swung the momentum and football game in the direction of Thomson. Cedartown produced no serious threat, and Thomson ate up most of the clock with a long fourth-quarter drive to seal the victory and the state championship at 27–7.

It was a sad ending to a year that had started with a lot of disappointment and ended with a spectacular attempt to conquer the football world. No one is ever satisfied with a loss, but the 1985 team never quit and gave all it had to give until the final gun sounded on a freezing night in Thomson, Georgia.

Allen Price and Van Dingler were named to the 1985 *Atlanta Journal-Constitution* all-state team.

1986

The intensity level was at a fever pitch as the Bulldogs prepared for the 1986 football season. Never mind that stars like Allen Price and Van Dingler had moved on and left Hill and his staff in a rebuilding year. Everyone knew that Coach Hill and his staff would develop the younger players and have them ready to compete for the region and, hopefully, make another run at a state championship. What no one counted on was a tough bunch of boys from Villa Rica who had grown tired of the yearly thumping put on them by the likes of Carrollton and Central of Carrollton.

Nevertheless, Hill had brought up some young stars like running backs Lawayne Ridgeway and John Barrow. Chad Smith and Skip Benton staged a heated battle for quarterback, with Smith getting the call as starter, but Benton would also get plenty of playing time. All-star-caliber linemen James Atkins and Casey Puckett anchored the defense.

The excitement swelled as the undefeated Central of Carrollton Lions came to town. The Lions from the AA ranks had already knocked off Villa Rica and Carrollton and possessed a balanced attack of running and passing the football. Everything was going right for the 'Dogs in the first quarter as they controlled the ball on the ground and punched it in for a 7–0 lead. In the second quarter, the Lions went to the air. With lightning-quick strikes aided by a Cedartown fumble, Central of Carrollton took a 21–7 lead into halftime. It was all they needed, as the second half turned into a barrage of fumbles and interceptions. The ferocious defense swarmed the Cedartown backfield, held Ridgeway and Barrow in check and didn't allow either Cedartown quarterback time to pass.

The midseason bye week came just in time to let Hill and his staff prepare a game plan for another tough team—the Villa Rica Wildcats. As injuries began to mount, the coaching staff needed the extra week to bring in younger players to fill the depleted roster.

Since the opening loss to Central of Carrollton, Villa Rica had smashed its opponents by a combined score of 205–21 in four games. It didn't take Villa Rica long to get its speedy offense in motion. Late in the first quarter, Marcus Holliday broke free for a forty-seven-yard touchdown run. Early in the second quarter, Santray McCoy sprinted into the end zone from twenty-five yards out. Cedartown came back with a long drive that stalled on the ten-yard line. Gaining momentum, the 'Dogs held the Wildcats and forced them to punt. The snap from center sailed over the punter's head and was kicked out of the end zone for a safety to make the score 14–2 at the half.

Cedartown took possession to begin the third quarter and put Villa Rica back in the driver's seat when Smith's pass was intercepted and ran back to the Cedartown nineteen-yard line. The 'Dogs' defense stiffened, but the Wildcats were able to score the touchdown to make the score 21–2. In the fourth quarter, Lawayne Ridgeway took a handoff up the middle and ran around, through and over Wildcat defenders for a sixty-three-yard touchdown. For one moment, the Bulldog nation and the Wildcats were reminded of what it meant to be a Cedartown Bulldog, as Ridgeway displayed the courage, the heart and the desire that go into a Cedartown football uniform. Old hard hitters like Tony Camarata, Dippy Wyatt, Dutch Foster and Ed Wilkes would have been so proud to see this young fellow carry on the tradition in 1986.

However, the 21–9 loss was a big setback for Cedartown's goals of winning the region title and making a state championship run. With Carrollton waiting in the wings, it was time for the 'Dogs to stand up and play their best football.

Fortunately for Cedartown, Carrollton was having a bad year. Coming into the game with the Bulldogs, the Trojans were 2-3-1, but they were still Carrollton. It was a slippery field and a rain-soaked football, as the overland path was the best way to travel when the Bulldogs and Trojans squared off. Ridgeway picked up where he had left off, battling and bruising defenders as the Bulldogs went out to a 6–0 first-quarter lead. Carrollton answered Cedartown's touchdown in the second quarter and made the extra point to go ahead 7–6. The third quarter bogged down, and no one offered a scoring threat. In the fourth quarter, the 'Dogs put together a long drive that led to John Barrow kicking a twenty-seven-yard field goal to give Cedartown the 9–7 victory.

If Cedartown couldn't win the region, it could still make the playoffs and have a chance at the state title by being the sub-region runner-up, but that wasn't going to be easy. Standing in front of it were the undefeated LaFayette Ramblers and a history of big plays and broken hearts. Cedartown scored in the first quarter to go up 7–0. The Bulldog defense dominated the Ramblers throughout the game. Several times, the 'Dogs drove the ball into LaFayette territory to see the drive come to an end because of a turnover or a costly penalty.

With less than four minutes remaining in the game, Cedartown recovered a fumble on the Rambler twenty-six-yard line. Two plays later, LaFayette's David Shuttles picked up a Cedartown fumble and was headed for pay dirt until Chad Chandler caught him from behind at the Cedartown twenty-five-yard line. On third down, Cedartown's defense threw the quarterback for a nine-yard loss. On fourth down, Craig Ramsey, scrambling for his life, heaved a desperation pass to Randy Southern for a first down at the ten-yard line. Three plays later, Michael Fairbanks punched it in from the four to make the score Cedartown 7, LaFayette 6. Going for the win, LaFayette ran a sweep around the right side to give the Ramblers the 8–7 victory and eliminate Cedartown from region competition.

The next week, Villa Rica ended LaFayette's run by a score of 40–13. The Villa Rica Wildcats gave the Dalton Catamounts their only loss of the season as they won the region championship. The Wildcats went on to win the 1986 AAA state championship.

Central of Carrollton lost to Adairsville the week after the Lions beat Cedartown. They would not lose again and were the 1986 AA state champions.

1987

With Ridgeway at fullback, Smith at quarterback and a host of outstanding offensive players returning, Cedartown looked to the defense to solidify a promising '87 season. The intensity from the '85 championship had settled down, but everyone knew that Hill and company had another special team that would compete for the region championship.

Cedartown had climbed the *Atlanta Journal-Constitution* AAA poll to the No. 6 position. With a record of four wins and no losses, the 'Dogs were preparing for a rematch with the undefeated defending AA champions from Central Carrollton. While the Lions held a tight hold on the No. 1 ranking in AA, they also achieved national recognition by attaining the *USA Today* No. 20 national ranking.

While installing his game plan, Hill knew that the key to beating the Lions was stopping the running of Walt Crowder and the passing of quarterback Mark Holt. Playing with tenacity and heart, the Bulldogs were able to keep it close for most of the game, but the strength of Crowder and the arm of Holt were too much as Central pulled ahead and won 35–21.

There was no time to lick the wounds from the last battle because that Wildcat up in Villa Rica was waiting for the 'Dogs to come up and see who was in control of the region. Villa Rica's season had been a little bit up and down. After losing a tough battle to Central of Carrollton and a one-point thriller to Campbell of Fairburn, the Wildcats rebounded to beat a very good Etowah team but had only slipped from No. 1 to No. 2 in the AAA poll.

Knowing that the Wildcats were vulnerable, Hill sent his 'Dogs out for the battle. Cedartown drove the ball deep into Wildcat territory but was stopped when Chad Smith's pass was intercepted in the end zone. The Wildcats went right to work. Quarterback Harold Keller tossed a fifty-yard scoring pass to Chuck Bishop to put Villa Rica in front 7–0. With a minute left in the first quarter, Chad Chandler received a punt on his fifteen-yard line and returned it to the Villa Rica four-yard line. Three plays later, Lawayne Ridgeway scored to even the score at 7–7.

In the second half, Cedartown threatened to score as it moved the ball to the Villa Rica nine-yard line. The Wildcats dodged the bullet when Smith was once again intercepted. On the move, the 'Dogs had just crossed midfield when Smith was stripped of the ball and Villa Rica recovered on the forty-one-yard line. A twenty-yard pass moved the ball to the twenty-one-yard line. Two plays later, Stanley Nalls bullied his way in from the fifteen. The kick for the extra point was blocked, and Villa Rica held a 13–7 lead.

The next team on the schedule was the Carrollton Trojans. Although the loss to Villa Rica was costly, it didn't eliminate the 'Dogs from the playoff hunt. A win against Carrollton would put Cedartown on track for a berth in the region playoffs. Behind the running of Lawayne Ridgeway and David Pace, the passing of Chad Smith to receivers Jon Anderson and Gabriel Harris and pure determination, Cedartown surged ahead in overtime to defeat Carrollton 43–27.

Wins over Chattooga, LaFayette and Cass put the 'Dogs in another match with Dalton. Along the way to the playoffs, Cedartown was faced with an unusual situation as a newsbreak in the *Rome News Tribune* made an insinuation that because of his birth date, Lawayne Ridgeway was too old to play high school football. Coach Hill answered by sending copies of birth certificates of every player on the team to the Georgia High School Association. The GHSA responded by announcing that every player on the Cedartown team was eligible to play the entire season.

Ridgeway ran the opening kickoff to the thirty-five-yard line. The 'Dogs drove to Dalton's forty-five-yard line and were forced to punt. Jon Anderson's punt rolled dead at Dalton's two-yard line. On the first play from scrimmage, Dalton fumbled, and Cedartown recovered on the four-yard line. It took four plays for Ridgeway to pound the ball in for a 7–0 Cedartown lead.

In the second quarter, Dalton won the battle of field position and drove thirty-three yards to score a touchdown. The missed extra point left the score at Cedartown 7, Dalton 6. Late in the quarter, Cedartown drove the ball to the Dalton twenty-three-yard line, but Smith's pass was intercepted in the end zone to end the threat. After an exchange of punts and fumbles, Dalton went to work from its twenty-yard line. Mixing the run and pass, the Catamounts needed only eight plays to find the end zone. The failed attempt for the 2-point conversion put Dalton in front 12–7.

Cedartown came storming back on the arm of Chad Smith as Ridgeway capped the drive with a spectacular one-handed catch for the touchdown. After another missed extra point, the 'Dogs led 13–12. The Catamounts quickly answered with a four-play drive that culminated with Dawson taking a pitchout and running for thirty-nine yards for the score. The 'Dogs began to move the football until Chad Smith was thrown for a sixteen-yard loss. On fourth down, Smith's pass was intercepted to end the Bulldogs' hopes for a championship season.

Lawayne Ridgeway was named to the 1987 *Atlanta Journal-Constitution* all-state team.

1988

Hill faced many challenges in 1988. None was greater than finding a quarterback to replace two-year starter Chad Smith. Brian Burgdorf had shown a lot of accuracy and arm strength in practice but had no real game experience. Hill would have top-notch receivers Chad Chandler, Paul Parsegian and Cassius Clay. David Pace and Kenny Weaver returned for their senior seasons at running back and would run behind a young, inexperienced offensive line. Hill was confident that his defense would come around, but like the offensive line, they had some growing up to do.

The 'Dogs looked like they would all grow up in a hurry as they handled Rockmart 29–8. Coach Hill said that the Bulldogs played one of the best games they had played since he had been coaching in Cedartown.

The next week in Fort Payne, Alabama, the 'Dogs weren't so impressive as the defense allowed the Wildcats to ramble for 340 yards on the ground and surge to a 37–20 victory. Weaver gained 140 yards on the ground, and Brian Burgdorf completed seven out of fourteen passes for 134 yards. Hill said that he was disappointed that the Fort Payne linemen were able to knock the Cedartown defenders off the ball.

A delay of game penalty that was called on Cedartown before the game began set the atmosphere for the game against Murray County. The Bulldogs never were able to pick up the tempo and lost a game on a sloppy field in overtime by the penetration rule, 15–14.

Things didn't get much better two weeks later when the 'Dogs traveled to Dalton. The Catamount defense shut down Cedartown's offense and sent the Bulldogs home with a three-game losing streak and a place in the cellar of region 7AAA.

Finally, the defense came around and the offense prevailed in wins over Central of Carrollton and Chattooga, and Cedartown seemed to be back on track.

Anniston, Alabama, brought its brand of Bulldog to Cedartown and left Hill and his young pups wondering if this season would be salvageable. After taking a 28–14 lead into the locker room at halftime, the Bulldogs came out looking like a different team. Penalties, turnovers and injuries killed any momentum they would build in the second half as Anniston put up 21 unanswered points to steal a game that should have belonged to Cedartown.

After a 54–19 blowout of Cass, the stage was set for Cedartown and Carrollton to duke it out for the sub-region crown. Carrollton opened the scoring in the second quarter with a touchdown pass and missed the extra point for a 6–0 lead. On the first play of Cedartown's next possession, Burgdorf tossed a forty-yard pass to Paul Parsegian. Two plays later, he found Parsegian alone in the end zone for the touchdown. The extra point gave Cedartown a 7–6 lead. On the ensuing kickoff, Carrollton's Crowder returned the kick for an eighty-five-yard touchdown. The 2-point conversion was good to put the Trojans in the lead 14–7. Carrollton's forty-four-yard field goal put Carrollton in front 17–7 at the half.

A scoreless third quarter set up an eleven-play, eighty-yard drive that ended when Burgdorf sneaked in from a yard out. As the defense rose up and stopped Carrollton's vaunted offense, Cedartown's offense hit full stride. Taking over on its forty-seven-yard line, Cedartown used ten plays to find the end zone and take a 21–17 lead. The Bulldog defense fought tooth and nail to hold Carrollton out of the end zone, but with seconds remaining in the game, the Trojans punched the ball across the goal line to take the victory.

The last game of the season saw the Bulldogs revert back to the same type of error-filled football when the Central of Carrollton Lions came to Cedartown and put the final touches to John Hill's first losing season at Cedartown High School.

1989

Shedding off the first losing season of a coach's career has to be a painful ordeal. Sure, Cedartown was competitive in every game in 1987 and, with a little luck, could have won five or six games. However, the stigma of a losing season had fans wondering about the direction of the program. The participation numbers had made a significant drop in the last few years, and that wave of red jerseys covering the sidelines between the forty-yard lines didn't look as intimidating as it had when the Burger Brigade marched up and down Doc Ayers's field at Cedartown Memorial Stadium. Although he was concerned about the lack in numbers and experience, Coach Hill was excited that he had a hot-handed junior quarterback in Brian Burgdorf as the nucleus to build a dynamic offense. What he didn't know at the time was that he had a wide receiver, Myron Pace, who may have been the most athletic player to ever wear the red and black colors of CHS.

Myron Pace stood six feet, three inches tall and weighed 215 pounds. Hill discovered him on the basketball court when he was a slam-dunking sophomore. Myron had great hands that could grab an alley-oop pass and slam it through the basketball goal or gently lay it against the backboard. He had a vertical leap and hang time that rivaled Michael Jordan. College scouts and recruiters were already calling the Cedartown office to inquire about the future of Myron Pace. Pace was enthusiastic about playing football as he spent the '87 season on the B team learning about footwork and pass routes.

Early indications from spring and summer practice were that Myron had learned his lessons well and was ready to play with the varsity.

Offensive linemen Todd Deterding and Shane Lee joined tight end Cassius Clay as the only returning lettermen on the offense. Running backs James Dulaney, Laron House, Ricky Porter and Keith Washington were fresh up from the JV and were unproven. The defensive side of the ball had more untested talent in linebackers Brad Stallworth, Jeff Dingler, Kenny Deaton and Stephen Puckett. Linemen Terry Dulaney, Troy Carter and Courtney Hammock bolstered the middle, while John Wilson, Tyrone Glover, Jarvis Frazier and Tony Whatley anchored the end positions. Benji Fraizer, Chris Shifflett, Kevin Ellison, Derek Hammock, Jason Bussy and Ron Ray were the defensive backs. It was going to be mix and match as Coach Hill would have to interchange players between offense and defense to allow rest periods for players while keeping his strongest units on the field.

The 'Dogs traveled across Polk County to begin the season against a tough and determined Rockmart team that was returning many starters from the previous season's team that had gone as far as the North Georgia championship game before losing to Washington Wilkes. Coach Steve Cordle's Yellow Jackets had shown steady improvement since he took over the helm in '87. Early in the first quarter, Rockmart's Brian Culver hit Rodney Sanders for a 74-yard touchdown pass, and the Yellow Jackets never looked back as they handed the young Bulldogs a 38–13 loss. Brian Burgdorf had several passes dropped but still managed eighteen out of thirty pass attempts for 139 yards.

There was no time to sit around and lick their wounds for the Bulldogs because Fort Payne, Alabama's No. 3–ranked Wildcats were coming to town with their high-powered running attack that had gained 611 yards in the first two games.

Not having much luck running the ball against Rockmart, Coach Hill made a bold move by putting tight end Cassius Clay into the running back position. The strategy paid off as Clay caught two passes from Burgdorf and rushed three times in the first quarter. Driving for five first downs and 151 yards, the 'Dogs held a 14–0 lead and possession of the football at the break. A 31-yard pass completion was nullified by a pass interference call. Clay ran for 27 yards but fumbled the ball, which was recovered by Fort Payne. Four plays later, Fort Payne's quarterback, Ken Pendergrass, tossed a 32-yard touchdown pass to John Stewart.

The Bulldogs took the kickoff and drove to midfield and once again fumbled and turned the ball over to Fort Payne. A Pendergrass pass completion, aided by a personal foul penalty, set the Wildcats up at Cedartown's eighteen-yard line. Two plays later, Fort Payne scored to tie the game at 14. Cedartown was penalized on the ensuing kickoff and was forced to start from inside the ten-yard line. On the first play from scrimmage, another fumble set Fort Payne up inside the twenty-yard line. Three plays later, Fort Payne's Thomas McDaniel raced into the end zone from twelve yards out to put the Wildcats up 21–14.

With a minute left before halftime, Clay picked up a Fort Payne fumble and ran for the score to tie the game at 21–21. Fort Payne would not be content going into the locker room for halftime with the score tied. Pendergrass heaved a long pass that deflected off the Cedartown defender's fingertips and into the arms of Stewart for a seventy-one-yard touchdown pass. The point after was missed, and Fort Payne led 27–21 at the half.

By the third quarter, the tempo had been set, with Cedartown fumbling and Fort Payne capitalizing on the miscues to take a 35–21 lead. Late in the third quarter, Burgdorf and company regained their composure and drove sixty-five yards to pull to within range of a touchdown. Clay once again was the workhorse, catching three passes and breaking off a run of twenty-five yards. Pace added two receptions, including a six-yard touchdown pass from Burgdorf.

The 'Dogs defense hunkered down and forced Fort Payne to punt and was given a tremendous break when the ball traveled nineteen yards before rolling out of bounds. After converting two fourth-down plays, the Bulldogs handed the ball over to the Wildcats with just over three minutes left in the game. Pendergrass put the final touches on the Fort Payne victory when he broke free and ran eighty-three yards for the final score of the game.

Just when you believe things can't get any worse, they do. Still reeling from the emotional loss to Fort Payne, the Bulldogs were faced with playing a group of talented and fired-up Murray County Indians on a muddy field with a slippery, rain-soaked football. That old encumbrance of the missed extra point came back to haunt the 'Dogs as the Indians prevailed 7–6.

When your back is up against the wall and running isn't an option, the only thing you can do is fight. That's exactly what the Bulldog defense did for four quarters against the third-ranked Dalton Catamounts. Late in the fourth quarter, Cedartown took possession of the ball at the ten-yard line. Throwing passes to clutch receivers Pace and Clay, the 'Dogs moved down the field. A twenty-eight-yard pass to Courtney Hammock moved the ball to the twelve-yard line. A pass completion to Pace moved the ball to within inches of the goal line, where Brian Burgdorf carried it in to put Cedartown up 6–3. The missed extra point was of no concern, as the Bulldog defense held Dalton until time expired.

Cedartown's offensive power came to the forefront against Central of Carrollton, churning out 119 yards passing and 218 yards rushing. The Bulldog defense turned in another solid performance, holding the Lions to one touchdown in a 28–14 win.

Cedartown defeated Chattooga 48–6 but ran into a monster in Anniston that couldn't be slain. The Alabama Bulldogs gave the boys from Cedartown a good look at what it takes to be a champion by the score of 47–0.

An 18–9 victory over Cass set the 'Dogs up for a showdown with undefeated and No. 3–ranked Carrollton for control of region 7AAA South. Carrollton would be the fifth team that Cedartown had played that was ranked No. 5 or better and the fourth team that was undefeated. The Trojans had little trouble running their record to 8-0, as they had allowed only two touchdowns all season. Cedartown laid Carrollton's great scoring record to rest as they crossed the goal line four times, but it wasn't enough to bring down the Trojans. Carrollton secured the sub-region championship title by beating the 'Dogs 31–26.

In a replay of the '88 season, the Bulldogs were faced with a must-win rematch with Central of Carrollton. In another tough contest, Cedartown pulled out the victory and the runner-up spot for the region playoffs.

With a record of five wins and five losses, Cedartown looked to be easy fodder for the North Champion Ringgold Tigers, but it didn't take long for Cedartown to declare that it had come to play. On the Bulldogs' second possession, Burgdorf hit Tony Hudson with a fifty-five-yard touchdown pass. The Tigers answered with a thirty-yard scoring toss but missed the extra point and trailed the 'Dogs 7–6. In the second quarter, Ringgold drove the ball sixty-six yards to the CHS three-yard line. The Bulldogs' defense stiffened and held the Tigers to a field goal.

In the third quarter, trailing 9–7, Cedartown took over the ball at the thirty-seven-yard line. After converting a fourth down and inches, Burgdorf threw a thirty-four-yard touchdown pass to Pace. The 2-point conversion gave the 'Dogs a 15–9 lead. Grinding out all but four minutes in the fourth quarter, Ringgold drove seventy-three yards for a touchdown that put the Tigers back on top 16–15. With the clock winding down, runs by Clay and passes from Burgdorf to Pace moved the ball down to the Ringgold twelve-yard line. Coach Hill sent Bob Tracey in to attempt a twenty-five-yard field goal. The stadium was electric, as it had been all night. Pace crossed his arms as Clay kneeled down on one knee and began to pray. Tracey's kick had plenty of distance as it strayed toward the left upright. The ball hit the upright and careened inward through the goal posts to give Cedartown the 18–16 win and a rematch with Carrollton for the region championship.

When you're hot, you're hot, and Cedartown was just that as it jumped out to a 24–0 lead in the second quarter and held on to defeat Carrollton 24–21 and win the 7AAA championship. The game went from being a potential blowout to a last-minute nail biter as Trojan kicker Trey Clodfelter missed a twenty-seven-yard field goal that would have tied the game. The big play of the game was when Cedartown's Ron Ray returned a Carrollton fumble five yards for Cedartown's first touchdown.

Now sporting the new nickname "Wonder Dogs," Cedartown would take its potent offensive attack to Atlanta to face No. 1–ranked and undefeated Marist War Eagles. Marist ran a superlative wishbone attack behind an offensive line that had bulled over every team in its path. On defense, the War Eagles had not given up more than one touchdown in any game. When Coach Hill was asked if he was afraid of his team being intimidated by Marist, he responded, "No, they weren't in awe of Anniston and that team was better than Marist."

In a game that was virtually even in time of possession, first downs, offensive yardage and turnovers, Marist used its first three offensive drives to build a 21–3 lead that the Bulldogs could not overcome. Crossing the goal line twice, Cedartown's storybook season came to a close as the War Eagles prevailed 28–15.

Brian Burgdorf threw for 1,627 yards and twelve touchdowns. Cassius Clay ran for 949 yards and ten touchdowns. He caught thirty-five passes for 277 yards and one touchdown. Myron Pace caught sixty-eight passes for 893 yards and nine touchdowns. Brian Burgdorf and Myron Pace were named to the *Atlanta Journal-Constitution* all-state team.

CHAPTER 13

RECORD-BREAKING ERA

1990

With a new season came new expectations, new goals and different attitudes. During the previous season, Cedartown had been trying to rebuild from a losing season. In 1990, Cedartown began the season as the defending region champion with a top ten ranking and players who had already gained state and national recognition. Brian Burgdorf was picked as a pre-season all-American. Receiver Myron Pace and offensive lineman Troy Carter were listed in the top 100 Georgia recruiting prospects. There was much fanfare, and the outlook was bright as the Bulldogs prepared for the opening game against Rockmart.

For some reason, Rockmart's Coach Cordle moved on, leaving the team to Ronnie Crabtree. There was a noted difference in the intensity of the Rockmart team without Cordle, and it was reflected by the 20–8 Cedartown win.

Murray County put up a good fight before falling 23–16 to the 'Dogs.

John Hill knew that Coach Bill Chappell and his Catamounts would be ready to play when the Bulldogs traveled to play Dalton. In the previous encounter, the Cat had gotten caught napping as the Cedartown "sleeping giant" squeaked out a 3–0 win. This time, Dalton took the opening kickoff and drove seventy-three yards to put the Catamounts on the board. Cedartown's passing attack came alive in the second quarter as Burgdorf threw three passes to Pace for a combined fifty-four yards. James Dulaney carried the ball in from the eleven-yard line to tie the score at 7–7. Dalton answered with a sixty-three-yard scoring drive to take a 14–7 halftime lead.

During the halftime break is when the fireworks began—literally. As thunder and lightning shook the stadium, rain flooded the field, leaving trenches and bare spots that had to be repaired before the game could continue. After a fifty-five-minute delay, Dalton kicked off to Cedartown.

The Bulldogs drove to the Dalton fifteen-yard line before the drive was halted by a penalty. Later in the third quarter, the Bulldogs reached the Dalton one-yard line, where they gave the ball up on a fumble. Throughout the game, Burgdorf and company were able to move the ball down the field but stopped themselves with turnovers or penalties.

Cedartown fielded a Dalton punt at the seven-yard line, but a penalty forced them to begin the fourth quarter from the three-yard line. Dalton intercepted a Burgdorf pass at the twenty-seven-yard line and, five plays later, scored the touchdown. On two attempts, aided by a Cedartown penalty, Dalton could not score the extra point, leaving the score at Dalton 20, Cedartown 7.

Throwing the ball practically every play, Cedartown marched down the field for Dulaney to run for a three-yard touchdown. Scott Ray's kick for the extra point pulled the Bulldogs to within six points. Dalton's next drive stalled, and the Cedartown aerial attack resumed. Burgdorf capped the drive with a one-yard run to even the score. Since the days of Bucky Ayers and the narrow defeats to Rossville, Cedartown had been blessed with some great kickers, but the extra point in high school football is not automatic, although it can be dramatic. By not converting the extra point, Cedartown and Dalton ended regulation play tied 20–20.

Cedartown took the overtime kickoff and drove to the Dalton 27-yard line before surrendering it on downs. Dalton ran two plays, and the referees called the game because of an 11:30 p.m. curfew. Cedartown believed that it had won the game on the penetration rule by moving the ball closer to Dalton's goal line than Dalton had come to Cedartown's goal. The official ruling from GHSA was that the overtime period did not count because it is required that two five-minute overtimes be played before a game is official. The final score was Cedartown 20, Dalton 20. Brian Burgdorf threw forty-three passes and completed twenty-seven of them for 315 yards.

After disposing of Southeast Whitfield, Cedartown faced an old foe that was developing a new attitude when it called upon the upstart Pepperell Dragons. Former Dragon player and University of Georgia letterman Lynn Hunnicutt had been building a special team in Lindale and was ready to put it to the test against the Bulldogs. The Dragons were good enough and tough enough as they took advantage of Cedartown penalties and mistakes to take a 21–15 victory.

Not looking back, Cedartown ran off three straight wins before its showdown with Carrollton for control of region 7AAA. As always, the Trojans were a strong football team, having lost one game early in the season to Lovett. The Cedartown offense opened the game with a playbook perfect eighty-five-yard drive for a touchdown. The 2-point conversion put the 'Dogs ahead 8–0.

The Trojans gave the ball back to Cedartown when Benji Fraizer recovered a fumble. That set up a twenty-three-yard field goal by Scott Ray to increase the lead to 11–0. In the second quarter, Carrollton's Jermaine Johnson broke free for a forty-one-yard touchdown burst. The 2-point try was good, and the gap was closed to 11–8. A bad punt by Cedartown set up Carrollton's next score, and the 'Dogs found themselves trailing 15–11. With pinpoint accuracy, Burgdorf threw passes to Stuart Hackney, Dulaney and Keith Washington as Cedartown drove seventy-eight yards and regained the lead on a twenty-seven-yard touchdown pass to Pace.

The only scoring in the third quarter was a forty-two-yard field goal by Carrollton's Matt Mundy, which tied the contest at 18–18. After an exchange of punts, Carrollton took over the ball and drove sixty-seven yards to take a 25–18 lead with three minutes and thirty-seven seconds remaining to play.

Cedartown took possession of the ball at the twenty-yard line. All the Cedartown fans were looking at one another with wide grins on their faces. Down on the field wearing number 12 was the most heralded Cedartown quarterback of all time. There have been many great ones. Ted Peeples made a huge contribution to restoring the Cedartown tradition. Jeff Burger led his team to a phenomenal win-versus-loss record. Jimmy Carter's team won the only official state championship. Jerry Weaver came along when Doc Ayers's program was struggling and helped put it back on course. But on that cool November night, the quarterback standing on the field represented the personification of the Bulldog spirit. Like Weaver, Brian Burgdorf came along when the Bulldogs were struggling. He and a bunch of talented football players had put Cedartown back into the upper echelons of Georgia high school football. Now, as he stood over his team with eighty yards to go for the potential tying or winning score, everyone knew that if he could pull it off he would "punch his ticket" and go on to play for any college football team in America.

Passes to Pace and Hackney, fortified by runs from Washington and Dulaney, set up a third down and seven yards to go. Burgdorf took the snap at the twenty-one-yard line and dropped back to pass. Pace had run a post route and cut it back toward the corner of the end zone, where he found daylight between him and two Carrollton defenders. Burgdorf's pass was on the mark, and Pace pulled it in for the touchdown. It was brilliant! The young quarterback played some of his best football as he, in the words of Ed Barrett, "Led the Bulldogs to the Promised Land."

There is an old axiom in sports that says to go for the win on the road and go for the tie at home. Hill called for the 2-point conversion attempt as the CHS fans held their breath. Burgdorf handed the ball to Keith Washington on a dive play for the three-yard score. Leading 26–25, the 'Dogs wanted to keep Carrollton out of Matt Mundy's field goal range, which meant keeping the Trojans from reaching the Cedartown thirty-yard line. Mundy had already made one from forty-two yards, and the one minute and nine seconds left of play was plenty of time for the high-powered Carrollton offense to move the football to within Mundy's range.

Six straight pass completions by the Trojan "hurry-up" offense moved the ball over midfield and into Cedartown territory. Carrollton faced a fourth down and three yards to go with the ball on the thirty-three-yard line. Carrollton's coach, Ben Scott, sent Mundy onto the field to attempt a fifty-yard field goal. In the previous season, Scott had sent Mundy on to the field to attempt the critical field goal against Cedartown but called him back in favor of Trey Clodfelter. Clodfelter missed the kick that would have tied the game. It is doubtful that anyone who was in attendance had ever seen a high school player kick a game-winning fifty-yard field goal. Well, they saw it on that cool autumn night as Mundy's kick eased over the uprights by a couple of feet to give the Carrollton Trojans the 7AAA championship.

To Cedartown fans it was heart wrenching, but all the fans agreed that they had just seen one of the most exciting games of football that had ever been played on any level. Receiving post-game accolades from Coach Hill were Jarvis Fraizer, Terry Dulaney, Thomas Janes and Brad Stallworth.

The Carrollton game took a physical toll on the Bulldogs, and the Villa Rica Wildcats were the worst possible opponent for the 'Dogs to face. With eight Bulldogs players—including five starters—on the injured list, Villa Rica turned up the heat. When a defensive player slipped in and sacked Brian Burgdorf and injured his shoulder, it was the end of the season for Burgdorf and the Bulldogs as Villa Rica triumphed 29–17.

Cedartown and University of Alabama quarterback Brian Burgdorf. *Courtesy of Mrs. Rita Burgdorf.*

Carrollton lost in the semifinals to Worth County. Lynn Hunnicutt's Pepperell Dragons completed their quest for prominence by going undefeated and winning the 1990 Georgia AA state championship.

Myron Pace ended his Cedartown football career as the all-time leading receiver with 2,083 yards and eighteen catches for touchdowns. He was named to the *Atlanta Journal-Constitution* all-classification all-state team.

Brian Burgdorf broke every passing record in school history by completing 336 out of 597 passes for 4,661 yards and thirty-nine touchdowns. He also ran for 1,193 yards and twenty-two touchdowns. He was selected as the *Atlanta Journal-Constitution* AAA Player of the Year. He played college football for the Alabama Crimson Tide and backed up Jay Barker in 1992 when Alabama won the national championship. In 1994, Brian was named Most Valuable Player of the Gator Bowl after he threw two touchdown passes and ran for a 33-yard touchdown. Brian contributed his success to Coach Hill and especially to offensive coordinator Coach Milton Hunnicutt.

Coach Hunnicutt began his coaching career in 1971 and came to Cedartown from Camden County High with Coach Hill. Before coming to Cedartown, Hunnicutt had coached Stump Mitchell and Ricky Anderson, who went on to become running backs in the NFL, as well as other notable college players. His tradition of developing fine offensive players has continued in Cedartown, as there has been an endless number of players who received college scholarships to play football.

1991

There was no way that Coach Hill was going to replace Brian Burgdorf and Myron Pace, but that didn't mean the cupboard was bare and there wouldn't be a formidable team to put on the field in 1991. For ages there had been a continual band of young boys watching from the sidelines, waiting for the chance to wear the red and black.

Although the Cedartown uniforms were not very decorative, they offered a mystique about them that was easily identifiable among high school players, coaches and fans. There was no red or black on the solid silver helmet. The jerseys were either red with white numbers on the front, the back and the sleeves or white adorned with red numbers. There were also special black jerseys with the same simple markings that Coach Hill would let the players wear as a special reward for working hard as a team and playing as a unit. There was nothing fancy about the britches, which were the same as the helmet—entirely silver. Whenever opposing teams saw players wearing those uniforms running onto the field, they realized that they had an enormous fight on their hands.

Coach Hill began the '91 season with a small group of fifty talented players. He had few stars and little depth at every position. Making the best with what he had available, he went to the option offense with Benji Fraizer as his quarterback. The first time Fraizer touched the football, he rambled off the right side of the line for 55 yards before being tackled at the Rockmart 7-yard line. The third time he touched the ball, he rushed over the goal line to put Cedartown on top 6–0. Jeremy Hayes added the extra point to put the Bulldogs ahead for good. Fraizer would go on to carry the ball eighteen times for 125 yards. Marcus Turner, Stuart Hackney and Larry Neal added over 50 yards each as the "new look" Bulldogs caught the Yellow Jackets off guard and rolled to a 48–7 victory. Hayes, who had only begun kicking two weeks before the start of the season, hit six out of seven extra-point attempts.

Hayes's kicking proved to be the difference the next week as the 'Dogs escaped with a narrow 10–7 win over Murray County. Although the Indians outgained the Bulldogs in yardage, it was Cedartown's ability to hold on to the football and commit only one turnover to the Indians' three that was the difference in the game.

It had been three years since Dalton had won a game against Cedartown. The previous season's 20–20 tie had done nothing to erase the two upset losses at the paws of the Bulldogs. Although the Catamounts couldn't shut down the Cedartown offense, they were able to keep the 'Dogs out of the end zone as they handed Cedartown its first defeat by a score of 34–6.

Pepperell brought its No. 1 AA ranking and nineteen-game winning streak into Cedartown to take on the 'Dogs. A challenge from Coach Hill to his team brought a new intensity to the team that was evident, as the score was locked at 0 going into the final quarter. Cedartown scored first in the fourth quarter. After going for the first down on a fourth down and one foot to go, Fraizer ran the final twenty-one yards into the end zone to take a 7–0 lead. Pepperell returned the kickoff to the forty-one-yard line. Two plays later, Pepperell's quarterback, Will Drew, threw a forty-nine-yard touchdown pass to his brother, David Drew, to put the Dragons on the board. Drew then passed to Roberts for the 2-point conversion to give the Dragons the lead and the 8–7 win. Both coaches said that the game was one of the hardest-hitting games they had ever seen.

Following a three-game winning streak, the Bulldogs were anxious to host the No. 1 AAA–ranked Carrollton Trojans. With that fifty-yard field goal still fresh in their minds, the Bulldogs wanted a chance at revenge on the Trojans. Coach Hill used his wits to get into the minds of the Carrollton coaches and team when he opened the contest with an onsides kick. Cedartown recovered and drove to the Carrollton twenty-one-yard line, where Jeremy Hayes kicked a thirty-eight-yard field goal.

Carrollton fumbled on its first play from scrimmage, and the 'Dogs recovered. Six plays later, Hayes booted a twenty-seven-yard field goal to put Cedartown in front 6–0. Cedartown took possession in the second quarter and drove to the twenty-two-yard line, where Hayes kicked his third field goal, giving the Bulldogs a 9–0 lead. Carrollton scored a touchdown after Stewart Hackney blocked a punt and a Carrollton player picked up the ball and advanced it for the first down. Carrollton's fullback, Mike Higgins, threw a fullback option pass for the nineteen-yard touchdown, drawing Carrollton to within 2 points.

In the fourth quarter, the Bulldogs began a long, methodical drive from the fourteen-yard line. Aided by a Marcus Turner run of sixteen yards on fourth and two, the 'Dogs moved to the twenty-yard line, where Hayes kicked his fourth consecutive field goal to extend the lead to 12–7. On the first play of Carrollton's next possession, Shane Jolly fell on a Carrollton fumble, putting the 'Dogs in business at the Trojan forty-yard line. Stewart Hackney broke free on a reverse sweep and took the ball to the Carrollton thirteen-yard line, where Hayes added his fifth field goal to put the Bulldogs up 15–7.

Knowing that Carrollton's kickoff return men were also track and field sprinters with game-changing ability, Coach Hill elected to try another onsides kick. Hayes's kick bounced over the Carrollton players and into the arms of Marcus Turner at the Trojan forty-four-yard line. The Bulldog offense capitalized on the mistake and drove the distance to make the score 22–7. The mighty Trojans were not quite defeated as they drove the ball to the Cedartown one-yard line. On a sweep around the right side, Carrollton's Fred Shackleford was met head-on by a wall of Bulldogs and fumbled. Cedartown's Tyrone Glover picked up the ball and sprinted toward the end zone. Just as a Carrollton player hit him, he pitched the ball to Demetrius Love, who ran the rest of the way for the score, making the final score Cedartown 29, Carrollton 7. Jeremy Hayes's five field goals were the most any player has kicked in one game in Georgia high school football history.

The Bulldogs had the momentum, the pride and the belief that this year Villa Rica was not going to block the path to the region championship. For nearly four quarters, the 'Dogs fought tooth and nail with the Wildcats and hung on to a 1-point lead with one minute and eighteen seconds to go in the game. Recovering a fumble on Villa Rica's first play from scrimmage, Cedartown drove fifty yards to surge to a 7–0 lead. Villa Rica answered in the second quarter with a fifty-yard drive to tie the game.

Early in the fourth quarter, Jeremy Hayes kicked a twenty-six-yard field goal to give the 'Dogs a 10–7 advantage. The Wildcats drove toward the Bulldog end zone until Derek Hammock intercepted a pass that killed the drive. Once again on the drive, the Wildcats were halted at the nine-yard line after the Bulldog defense stopped them on downs.

Trying to run off as much time on the clock as possible and hang on to the football, Cedartown faced a fourth down on the two-yard line. Backed up to the end zone and nearly out of downs, Coach Hill took his best chance on taking a safety in the end zone and awarding Villa Rica two points. Now with a one-point lead, Jeremy Hayes was allowed a free kick opportunity from the twenty-yard line to give the ball back to Villa Rica— and give the Bulldog defense some running room. The grandstands and bleachers were buzzing with excitement as Hayes punted the ball out of the shadows of his goalposts.

Waiting at the forty-five-yard line was Villa Rica's electrifying Phillip "Pops" Johnson. Johnson caught the punt in full stride with his momentum moving forward and bolted straight down the field. He blazed past Cedartown defenders and into the Cedartown end zone to put the Wildcats in front for the first time in the game.

Because Cedartown, Villa Rica and Carrollton had identical region records, Cedartown was eliminated because of the tiebreaker rule about region play. The loss to Dalton, a team Villa Rica and Carrollton had not played, was the reason Cedartown was eliminated. The team that played the toughest schedule was sent home. Villa Rica went on to lose in the state semifinals to Kendrick High School.

Offensive lineman Thomas Hanes, Jeremy Hayes and Benji Fraizer were all named to the *Atlanta Journal-Constitution* all-state team. Benji Fraizer went on to play football at Mars Hill College and returned to Cedartown to teach and coach football and basketball.

1992

A lack of depth and a lack of experience were the biggest obstacles that Hill and his Bulldogs had to overcome in a definite rebuilding year. To offset his lack of experienced football players, Coach Hill went out and scheduled two defending state champions in the first three weeks of the season. After the previous season's shellacking, Rockmart decided that it didn't want to play Cedartown and wouldn't provide any date that the Yellow Jackets would be available. Defending AA champion Cartersville was happy to step in and fill the opening-game slot. It is doubtful that the next team up, Fort Payne, Alabama, would be considered a breather before taking on AAA champ Kendrick.

Hill began the season with eight seniors on a squad of fifty-three players. Benji Fraizer was gone, and the quarterback position was the big question on everyone's mind. Getting the assignment for the start of the season was junior Adam Allen. Senior Marcus Turner would play some at quarterback and shoulder the load at running back.

On a rain-soaked field, the Bulldogs gave the Purple Hurricanes all they could handle and nearly pulled out the upset. Cartersville came from behind to take the 19–15 win.

Another valiant contest against Fort Payne saw the Bulldogs go down 26–18, but the ceiling fell in when Kendrick came to town and shut down the 'Dogs 26–0. Coach Hill reminded everyone that the Bulldogs were very young and better days were ahead.

Things got a little better when the 'Dogs picked up their first victory over Northwest Whitfield. On the road at Dalton, Coach Hill made a daring decision when he sent freshman quarterback Lee Jolly in to relieve Adam Allen. It was the first time he had introduced a freshman quarterback this early in the season and definitely the first time he had played a freshman in a hostile environment against one of the best teams in the state.

Lee Jolly was no ordinary freshman; he was groomed for the role by one of Cedartown's best coaches, his father. His father was Coach Ken Jolly, who had grown up in Cedartown and played football and baseball for the Bulldogs. Kenny, as the Bulldog Nation knows him, went on to play college baseball for Birmingham-Southern College in Birmingham, Alabama. In his senior year, he was voted all-conference and all–District 27 and all–Area IV as a pitcher. After graduation, he signed a professional baseball contract with the Philadelphia Phillies. Kenny is one of the unsung heroes in Cedartown athletics who excelled as a teacher and a coach. His philosophy to the young players was, "Believe in what we're doing and give your best effort." One highlight of his career was when he coached the Cedartown Lady Bulldogs basketball team all the way to the state quarterfinals.

If there was going to be any luster in the game for young Lee Jolly, it wasn't going to be in his first start against Murray County. Two weeks earlier, the Indians had edged Dalton by 1 point and had rolled over Ringgold. They kept pressure on Jolly by sacking him six times and forced three interceptions. Undeterred, in the third quarter, Jolly threw a sixty-three-yard completion to freshman Cedric Clark to get the ball to the five-yard line and showed everyone why he was now the Bulldog quarterback when he scrambled out of the pocket and dove over for the score that tied the game 6–6. The high-powered Indians would not be denied as they went on to win 20–6.

Demetrius Love rushed for 215 yards on twenty-five carries and scored three touchdowns to lead the Bulldogs to a 40–27 win over Ridgeland.

In the next game against Rome, Jolly began to shine as he and Love ran over the Wolves' defense for a combined 340 yards. In all, Cedartown's offense gained 424 yards and tamed the Wolves 41–7.

On a freezing night in a game that was marred by turnovers but dominated by the Cedartown defense, the Bulldogs defeated Ringgold 20–0 and earned a berth in the region playoffs. However, quarterback Lee Jolly left the game with a pulled groin injury, and his playing status was questionable for the next game.

With a playoff berth in hand, perhaps the 'Dogs lost their focus on their next opponent, or maybe the loss of Lee Jolly made a great difference to the team, as the Bulldogs were upset by Southeast Whitfield. With a record of four wins and six losses, they had to beat Dalton and win in the state playoffs to have any chance of a winning season.

With Marcus Turner at quarterback, the Bulldogs fought the Dalton Catamounts for one half before Dalton erupted for four unanswered scores to eliminate Cedartown from the playoffs and end the season.

1993

For the first time in several years, the Bulldogs had enough quality players that Coach Hill wouldn't have to play so many players on offense and defense. He believed that a key to success was to have players like Bryan Edge and Mike Worthington playing strictly defense while Shamus Salter and Leonel Cruz concentrated on offense. To make that possible, junior players Jonathan Stone, Jason Hogg and Jason Duggar were going to have to step up and meet the challenge. Dwayne House would be the starter at fullback, while a group of young but talented running backs battled for the starting halfback job. Adam Allen and Lee Jolly were fighting a heated battle for the starting quarterback position, which probably wouldn't be decided until the day of the game. Coach Hill said that both players would get playing time early in the season.

Penalties and turnovers handicapped the 'Dogs early in the opening contest against Cartersville. The solid defensive play kept the Hurricanes at bay until the second quarter, when Cartersville's Cedric Ward hit Larry Turner for a fifty-one-yard scoring strike. Cedartown quickly responded as Lee Jolly connected with Quentin Dulaney for a sixty-five-yard touchdown pass. Jeremy Hayes's kick for the extra point sailed wide right, and the Bulldogs trailed 7–6.

In the third quarter, Cedartown's Adam Allen put his mark on the game when he tossed a fifty-eight-yard scoring pass to Cedric Clark. The 2-point conversion attempt was unsuccessful, and the Bulldogs led 12–7. Cartersville, however, was not through as it mounted an eleven-play, seventy-two-yard drive that culminated with a ten-yard touchdown pass from Ward to Alan Callahan. Cartersville took a 15–12 lead on a successful 2-point conversion. The Bulldogs drove the ball to the Cartersville four-yard line but couldn't cross the goal line as Lee Jolly's second-down pass was tipped at the line of scrimmage and intercepted by Cartersville's Tim Greene.

Against Fort Payne, Cedartown built a 14-point lead on runs by Lee Jolly and Quentin Dulaney. The game and the momentum seemed to be well in hand until Lee Jolly's pass was intercepted by Seth Shankles and returned to the thirty-one-yard line. Four plays later, quarterback Tyler Griggs ran the ball in from the eight-yard line to put the Wildcats on the board. The Wildcats returned the favor when they fumbled the ball that was recovered by Cedartown at the seventeen-yard line. LaCraig Malone took the pitch and scored from the six-yard line to put the 'Dogs back on top 21–7. The Wildcats drove the ball fifty-nine yards and scored on a nineteen-yard pass from Griggs to Derek Kidd to pull to within a touchdown. On fourth and inches at the Wildcats' thirty-one-yard line, the Bulldog defense stiffened to stop the Wildcats and win their first game of the season.

In a defensive struggle, the Kendrick Cherokees defeated the Bulldogs by a score of 14–3. Despite giving up 253 yards on the ground, the Bulldog defense put forth a gallant effort as the Cherokees assaulted the Cedartown end zone throughout the ballgame.

Lee Jolly ran for 151 yards and two touchdowns to lead the 'Dogs to a 38–21 win over Northwest Whitfield. Jolly threw a touchdown pass to Cedric Clark, and Quentin Dulaney added another score as the offense accounted for 333 yards.

Bill Chappell brought his sixth-ranked and undefeated Catamounts to Cedartown and ran into a buzz saw as the Bulldogs surged to a 14–0 lead. Lee Jolly kept the ball on the option play and raced for a fifty-eight-yard score to put the 'Dogs up 7–0. Revealing his big play potential for the first time, Dulaney fielded a punt at the eight-yard line, shook off a Dalton defender and ran ninety-two yards for the score.

In the third quarter, Dalton put together a ten-play, sixty-two-yard drive and scored on quarterback Benji McConkey's five-yard run. The Catamount defense held and took over at the Cedartown forty-eight-yard line. Eight plays later, McConkey took the ball over from the one. After a Mike Worthington interception, Cedartown drove to the Catamount twenty-eight-yard line, where Jeremy Hayes put the 'Dogs in front 17–14 with a forty-five-yard field goal. Dalton's McConkey threw a fifty-one-yard pass completion to Charlie Bethel and then ran it in from the five-yard line to put the Catamounts ahead 21–17. The Bulldogs' ensuing drive was stopped at the fifty-yard line, preserving the win for Dalton.

It was a somber outing for the Bulldogs when they had to face the Murray County Indians without offensive guard and defensive tackle Leonel Cruz. Leonel wasn't with the team because he was in Mexico mourning the loss of his mother and father, who were killed in an automobile accident.

The 'Dogs responded with a solid defensive effort that didn't allow the Indians to penetrate the end zone. Quentin Dulaney ran down Murray County's Glen Owensby from behind to stop one score. Shae Ledbetter intercepted a pass in the end zone, and the Cedartown defense held firm when Murray County advanced the ball to within inches of the goal. An Indian thirty-one-yard field goal was the only points the Dog Day defense would allow. Lee Jolly tossed a short pass to Dulaney, who turned the pitch into a fifty-four-yard touchdown to give Cedartown the 7–3 victory. Afterward, in the locker room, the team dedicated the game to Leonel Cruz.

Quentin Dulaney's sixty-four-yard run for a touchdown highlighted Cedartown's 24–13 win over Rome.

Once again, Dulaney gave the 'Dogs an early spark with a seventy-three-yard punt return for a touchdown. Later in the first quarter, Dulaney left the game with a knee injury that would sideline him for at least two weeks. Jolly, Cedric Clark and LaCraig Malone picked up from there and led the 'Dogs to a 42–13 win over Ringgold.

With a dominating defense, Cedartown clinched second place in the region and home field advantage in the first round of the playoffs by defeating Southeast Whitfield 40–7.

With the return of Quentin Dulaney and a thundering pass rush, Cedartown easily handled Northwest Whitfield 42–16 and advanced to the state playoffs.

In a driving rain and sloppy field, Cedartown took on the undefeated and sixth-ranked Clarkston Angoras. In a scoreless ballgame in the second quarter, Roderick Turner let a slippery punt get away from him, and Clarkston recovered it deep in Cedartown territory. When Sean Henry exploded through the left side of the line for a touchdown, Clarkston seized the momentum and never gave it up. Two minutes later, Tyrone Lewis blocked Jeremy Hayes's punt, and Mike Lucky recovered it in the end zone, putting the Angoras up 14–0. On its next possession, Cedartown failed to convert a fourth-down attempt and turned the ball over to Clarkston. Two plays later, Henry rambled for a thirty-eight-yard score. Clarkston's defense recorded its sixth shutout of the season and eliminated Cedartown from the playoffs by a score of 28–0. Coach Hill credited Clarkston's defense for not allowing the 'Dogs to get the ball to the corner of the line of scrimmage where their speedy backs had play-breaking ability.

Jeremy Hayes and Brian Edge were named to the 1993 *Atlanta Journal-Constitution* all-state team.

1994

With thirteen returning starters—including a fast quarterback, a running back capable of scoring anytime he touched the ball, hard-hitting defenders and a supporting cast of seasoned football players—Cedartown began the

1994 season ranked third in the *Atlanta Journal-Constitution* poll. Returning starters were Shae Ledbetter, La Craig Malone, Jonathan Stone, Jason Hogg, Kevin Boozer, Roderick Turner, Jason Duggar, Bryan Holland, Dwayne House, Cedric Clark, Tex Tumlin, Quentin Dulaney and Lee Jolly.

Spring practice for 1994 presented a new challenge for Coach Hill and his staff. Out of seventy-three players, thirty of them were eighth graders who would be freshmen in the fall. Practices and drills would have to be tailored to meet the needs of veteran starters and youngsters who had never played in a varsity game. The situation did hinder the progress of the older players, but having them there as models and guides helped the freshmen learn the system much faster. The first week of practice was devoted entirely to basic fundamentals like foot position and blocking technique. Realizing the immense potential in these eighth graders, Coach Hill was not about to let them start out off course because he knew that the time he invested would pay dividends in the near future.

When the bell sounded to start the '94 season, Cedartown broke out of the gates like a sprinting quarter horse and went wire to wire as it defeated the LaFayette Ramblers 40–0. The Jolly/Dulaney duo accounted for most of Cedartown's 353 yards as the defense held the Ramblers to 99 yards. On Monday morning, the Cedartown Bulldogs were the No. 1–ranked AAA team in the state of Georgia.

The 'Dogs went on to win their next six games, including four shutouts, to set up a slugfest with undefeated and fourth-ranked Dalton. Cedartown's defense began the game hitting hard and furious, but a gutsy call by Dalton's coach, Bill Chappell, put the Catamounts on the board first. Going for a first down on fourth and inches, Dalton running back Peter Putnam broke free and scampered forty-two yards for the touchdown. Dalton missed the 2-point conversion and led 6–0. Cedartown fought back and drove the ball to Dalton's twenty-three-yard line before a fumble killed the drive.

In the second quarter, Dalton's Ty Macon scored on a thirty-two-yard run. Benji McConkey threw to Ricky Hammondtree for the 2-point conversion to extend the Catamount lead to 14–0. After a Dalton missed field goal, Lee Jolly broke loose on a sixty-six-yard touchdown run. Jeremy Cobb's kick for the extra point pulled the Bulldogs to 14–7. A short kickoff aided Dalton as it moved quickly down the field to score on McConkey's twenty-nine-yard touchdown run. The failed 2-point conversion gave Dalton a 20–7 halftime lead.

Cedartown took the second-half kickoff and drove sixty-six yards to cut the margin to 20–14. Late in the fourth quarter, Cedartown moved the ball into Dalton territory, but a fumble at the thirty-three-yard line ended the Bulldog drive and sealed the Catamount victory.

Dalton's Chappell said that the key to their win was to keep the ball out of the hands of Quentin Dulaney and diminish Cedartown's big play scoring threat. The plan proved to be successful, as Dulaney had nineteen yards rushing and no long kick returns.

Second place in the region and home field advantage was on the line when Cedartown hosted Murray County. Cedartown wasted no time getting control of the game by scoring twenty-two points in the first quarter.

The next game against Rome had no significance other than to claim the dominance in a long-standing rivalry. The Bulldogs had 415 yards of offense as they exploded against the Wolves by a score of 61–9. This was a fitting way for Coach Hill to get his 200th career win.

Cedartown finished the regular season with nine wins and one loss, which was good enough for second place and the right for a rematch at home with Murray County and a chance to make it to the state playoffs. In what Coach Hill called their best game of the year, the Bulldogs shut down the Indians 28–7. Lee Jolly rushed for 156 yards, which put him over 1,000 yards for the season. Quentin Dulaney gained 48 yards and also passed the 1,000-yard mark.

The first round in the playoffs put No. 5–ranked Cedartown against a familiar foe: the No. 6–ranked Marist War Eagles. Marist came into the game on a ten-game winning streak and had outscored its opponents by an average of 24–10. By applying defensive pressure in the middle of the line and securing the corners, Marist was able to contain the triple option. Marist's tackles kept pressure on Jolly, and the linebackers penetrated the backfield and tackled Dulaney whenever he took the pitchout. Whenever Jolly tried to pass, he was either sacked or hurried by the Marist defense.

After Marist scored on its first possession, the Cedartown defense responded and kept the War Eagles out of the end zone until the fourth quarter. After recovering a Marist fumble at the thirty-six-yard line on the last play of the quarter, Jolly fumbled the ball into the end zone, and Cedartown's Tex Tumlin recovered it.

In the third quarter, Marist drove the ball deep into Cedartown territory but fumbled away the scoring threat as Cedartown recovered at the twelve-yard line. Unable to run the ball, Jolly dropped back into the end zone and threw an incomplete pass. The referees ruled that he had intentionally grounded the pass and awarded Marist a safety, making the score Marist 9, Cedartown 7.

Jolly's free kick gave Marist possession at the Cedartown forty-one-yard line. On the second play, Marist's Bryan Davidson threw a forty-three-yard touchdown pass to Ryan Malec. Marist carried the momentum into the fourth quarter and shut down the Cedartown offense. The Bulldog defense that had been stubborn all night began to tire and gave up to long drives for War Eagle touchdowns as Marist prevailed 30–7.

Lee Jolly, Quentin Dulaney, Cedric Clark and Kevin Boozer were named to the 1994 *Atlanta Journal-Constitution* all-state team. The Atlanta Touchdown Club honored Coach Hill for joining an elite group of coaches who have won two hundred or more football games. Among those coaches are Max Bass (Cedartown assistant under Doc Ayers), Nick Hyder (West Rome/Valdosta), Bill Chappell (Dalton), Charlie Grisham (Carrollton), French Johnson (Rockmart) and Luther Welch (Thomson).

1995

The Bulldogs began the season on the road against LaFayette and found themselves in a tussle with the Ramblers until Andre Clark returned a second-quarter kickoff 92 yards for the touchdown. Running back Ray Williams rushed for 192 yards. An interesting play developed when Cedartown had the ball on the 20-yard line. Keeping the ball on the option, quarterback Lee Jolly ran for 25 yards before he tossed the ball to Williams, who ran for the score. The Bulldogs hammered out 314 yards on the ground as they defeated the Ramblers 40–0.

Gordon Central brought a determined group of football players to Cedartown with the intentions of upsetting the highly ranked Bulldogs. The Warriors were well equipped with big linemen and matched the Bulldogs pound for pound on the line of scrimmage. Cedartown's heralded rushing attack was held to 173 yards. Jolly was inefficient in the passing game as he completed five of fourteen passes for 54 yards. Gordon Central found the going just as rough but was able to pick up 196 yards, mostly through the air.

In the second quarter, Cedartown forced the Warriors to punt from the eleven-yard line. A short punt set the 'Dogs up at the thirty-seven-yard line. Lee Jolly threw a pass to Reggie Poole, and the big tight end rambled to the twenty-four-yard line. Two plays later, Jolly found Andre Clark at the goal line to score the first touchdown of the game. Jeremy Cobb's kick for the extra point put Cedartown in front 7–0.

The defensive struggle continued until early in the fourth quarter, when Warrior Jimmy Pope streaked down the sideline and pulled in a pass for a seventy-two-yard touchdown. On the extra point attempt, Gordon Central was called for illegal motion and penalized five yards. On the next attempt, a high snap from center resulted in a missed kick that turned out to be the difference in the game as Cedartown prevailed 7–6.

Now the No. 3–ranked AAA team in the state, the Cedartown football team was riding a wave of confidence—or overconfidence. It must have been the latter because the Ridgeland Panthers upset the high and mighty Bulldogs by a score of 28–22. Slowing down the Cedartown running game and shutting down the passing game, the Panthers played error-free football to pull off the upset. Cedartown gave away the football too freely with two lost fumbles and three pass interceptions.

Ridgeland never trailed in the game and had a 28–7 lead with two minutes and thirty-eight seconds remaining in the game. Cedartown put together a nine play seventy-yard drive to bring the score to 28–14. Andre Clark recovered Shiron Colvin's onside kick. On the next play, Clark caught a forty-five-yard touchdown pass from Jolly to pull the Bulldogs to within a touchdown, but Ridgeland recovered Colvin's next attempt at the onside kick. Coach Hill commented that the best team won the football game and that the Bulldogs had a lot of work to do to reach their potential.

After the Ridgeland loss, Coach Hill took over the helm and righted the course as the 'Dogs ran off six straight wins to set up a rematch with Ridgeland.

Playing a different brand of football, Cedartown went to the passing game for three touchdowns as the defense held Ridgeland in check. Lee Jolly threw two touchdown passes to Ronnie Spurgeon before leaving the game with an injured ankle. Backup quarterback James Hooper came in and threw a scoring strike to Reggie Poole as Cedartown improved its record to 10-1 to become the 7AAA region champions.

Cedartown hosted Marist in the first round of the state playoffs. It had been a while since the War Eagles had traveled to Cedartown, and Coach Hill was eager to see how his team responded to the home field advantage. Both teams went onto the field with a lot of intensity. As the War Eagles took the field, they taunted the Bulldogs by running along the Bulldog sideline with their hands extended and index fingers pointing out like they were waving pistols.

On the first play from scrimmage, Marist ran a flea flicker that resulted in a fifty-seven-yard completion from Joe Winland to Mike Hughes. Two plays later, Marist scored a touchdown to take a 7–0 lead. On Cedartown's first possession, Lee Jolly's pass was intercepted by Winland and returned for a thirty-seven-yard touchdown, and Marist had a 14–0 lead. Once again, Marist gained possession of the ball and drove to the Cedartown twenty-one-yard line, but James Malone stripped the ball from the Marist runner to stop the drive.

Early in the second quarter, Jolly dropped back to pass and threw a perfect pass to Ronnie Spurgeon as he bolted past the Marist cornerback and streaked down the sideline and ran all alone for a sixty-five-yard touchdown. On the first play of Marist's next possession, Andre Clark recovered a fumble, giving the 'Dogs the ball at the thirty-four-yard line. On the next play, Jolly hit Clark in stride as he ran between the Marist safeties for the touchdown. Marist rose to the occasion and blocked the point after kick to hang on to a 14–13 lead.

Midway in the third quarter, Cedartown recovered a Marist fumble and was in business at the Marist forty-yard line. Clark gained ten yards on an end around and then hauled in a pass from Jolly for eleven yards. Jolly then connected with Reggie Poole over the middle near the goal line. Poole carried the Marist defenders the last three yards for the touchdown. On the 2-point conversion attempt, Jolly flipped the ball to James Hooper, who threw a pass to Poole for the 2 points, giving Cedartown a 21–14 lead. Marist took the kickoff and drove sixty-five yards to tie the score at 21.

The Bulldogs drove the ball to the Marist fifteen-yard line, where Cobb put the 'Dogs back in front 24–21. Marist drove the ball to Cedartown's twenty-nine-yard line, but the drive was killed when Chad Ledbetter made a game-saving interception in the end zone.

Cedartown couldn't move the ball and was forced to punt with 9.7 seconds remaining in the game. Marist's Andrew Kerr called for the fair catch at the thirty-five-yard line. The Cedartown defender didn't see the signal for the fair catch and hammered the punt receiver. A fifteen-yard penalty was called against Cedartown and the ball was moved to the twenty-yard line. The rule in football is that after a team calls for a fair catch, it has an option for a free kick for a field goal. That meant that Cedartown would have to remove its players from the field while Marist attempted the field goal. Marist invoked that rule and sent the kicker and the holder onto the field to attempt a thirty-yard field goal. Everyone in the stadium stood frozen in time as that young teenager kicked the ball that didn't come close to the goal posts. In another thriller, Cedartown defeated one of its fiercest rivals and advanced to the next round in the playoffs.

It was a mystical evening at the Hart County football stadium the night the Hart County Bulldogs played the Cedartown Bulldogs in the state playoffs. The stadium was decked out in its usual orange and black school colors, but on this night, the hue from a big autumn moon gave the stadium an orange glow. The tight symmetry of the stadium packed with bundled-up fans gave it the resemblance of a small college stadium.

Hart County quarterback Ben Leard came into the game having completed 62 percent of his passes for more than 2,400 yards. However, Cedartown's Ken Veal, Geoffrey Fraizer, Reggie Poole and the rest of the Bulldog defense pressured Leard, sacking him eight times and holding him to 111 yards passing. Neither team was able to find the end zone as the first half ended in a scoreless tie.

Hart County took the second-half kickoff and began to move the football. Pushing Hart County back to the thirty-two-yard line, the 'Dogs seemed to have stalled the drive. On third down and fifteen, Leard hit Adam Brown for a twenty-three-yard completion and a first down. On the next play, Leard passed to Titus Johnson for a thirty-seven-yard touchdown to put Hart County on the scoreboard. The kick for the extra point was missed, making the score Hart County 6, Cedartown 0.

The Bulldogs went to the power running game using their superior size on the line and pounded the ball in the middle with Ray Williams, LaJuan Hoke and Isaac Schofield. The 'Dogs moved the ball to the Hart County thirty-five-yard line, but an illegal procedure penalty stopped the drive. Late in the third quarter, Cedartown drove to the Hart County twenty-eight-yard line but was stopped by a pass interception.

With six minutes and fifty seconds remaining in the game, Cedartown took over at the thirty-eight-yard line. Once again, the Bulldogs were able to move the ball. With just over two minutes to go and the ball on the Hart County fourteen-yard line, Cedartown was faced with fourth down and six yards to go. Coach Hill put the fate of the game and the season on Lee Jolly. Jolly had not healed from the ankle injury he had suffered against Ridgeland, and his lameness was becoming more apparent throughout the game. Jolly dropped back and threw to Ronnie Spurgeon, who made a clutch catch in heavy traffic for a ten-yard gain. Two running plays inched the ball closer to the goal line. On third down, Jolly kept the ball and found the end zone for the score. Jeremy Cobb's kick was true, and Cedartown had the lead 7–6.

After the kickoff, Leard and company began to play toss and catch. After driving deep into Cedartown territory, Geoffrey Fraizer and Preston Sewell broke through the line and sacked Leard at the thirty-yard line. Facing third down and needing twenty yards to make the first down, Hart County attempted a halfback pass that was picked off by Jolly, who was making a rare appearance in the secondary.

The Bulldogs would now advance to the semifinals of the state playoffs against Josey High School in Augusta, Georgia. Josey received the opening kickoff, ran three plays and punted to Cedartown. On Cedartown's first play, LaJuan Hoke broke through the line for an eleven-yard gain. On the next play, Josey recovered a fumble at the Cedartown twenty-four-yard line.

Three plays later, Cedartown's Ken Veal recovered a Josey fumble at the three-yard line. After moving the ball out to the twenty-yard line, Cedartown fumbled and gave the ball back to Josey. Josey drove to the goal line, and on fourth down, Josey quarterback George Brown found Percy Bland in the end zone to put Josey up 7–0.

Cedartown fumbled the ensuing kickoff that set Josey up for another easy score. Early in the second quarter, Josey mounted a fifty-five-yard drive that was aided with an unsportsmanlike penalty on Cedartown to take a 21–0 lead. Later in the second period, Josey mounted a seventy-yard drive that took the life out of the Cedartown team.

Trailing 29–0, the 'Dogs opened the second half with a long drive to the Josey six-yard line, but Deon Grant's circus-like interception killed any chance the 'Dogs might have had to get back in the game. Josey's coach, John Starr, said that Cedartown was much better than the 49–0 score indicated and agreed that after the early fumbles, the youngsters from Cedartown lost their composure and were not able to recover.

Josey was a team of destiny. Deon Grant went on to play on the Tennessee Volunteers national championship team. He also won a Super Bowl ring playing for the New York Giants.

Andre Clark, Lee Jolly, Reggie Poole and Ken Veal were selected to the *Atlanta Journal-Constitution* all-state team. Lee Jolly went on to play football and baseball for the University of Alabama at Birmingham.

1996

Hill was faced with a new set of challenges for the 1996 season. The student enrollment numbers were down, and Cedartown made the move from the AAA classification to Class AA. The classification may have changed, but the schedule was almost identical to the previous season's. The big difference was that instead of the annual dog and cat fight between Cedartown and Dalton for region dominance, the Bulldogs would once again have to match up with Pepperell, Villa Rica and Carrollton. The school may have dropped one letter, but the competition in 6AA may have been tougher than 7AAA. Some sportswriters pointed to this region as being the toughest AA region in the state. The pollsters were giving the big and heavy Bulldogs a lot of respect; they ranked them as the No. 4 AA team in the state.

The '96 edition of Bulldog football had a different complexion than the recent teams that had possessed lightning speed that could strike from anywhere on the field. Big offensive lineman Bo Perry had the size and ability to create holes for running backs Odell Abram and Isaac Schofield. Quarterback James Hooper had varsity experience and had proven he could handle the offense. Ronnie Spurgeon was developing into a quality receiver, and Reggie Poole could be an offensive threat as he doubled at tight end and linebacker. On the defensive side, Poole would team up with linebacker James Malone and defensive end Ken Veal to give Cedartown one of the toughest inside running defenses and one of the most feared pass rushing attacks in the area.

Not wanting to renew the rivalry with Cedartown in the first game of the season, Rockmart deferred to the second half, so Coach Hill took his team on the road to play AAA's No. 4–ranked Dalton. He wanted to put this team laced with size and strength to an early test against an opponent that was difficult to handle and nearly impossible to beat on its home field.

The Bulldog defense proved its dominance of the Catamounts through most of the four quarters of play. Fifty times the Cats pounded the Bulldog line, managing to get 184 yards and one touchdown. When Jeremy Cobb missed the game-tying extra point in the fourth quarter, all the Catamounts had to do was run out the clock to give Dalton the 7–6 win. On second down, Dalton fumbled the football, and LaJuan Hoke recovered to give the Bulldogs one last chance. With one minute and two seconds left in the game, James Hooper completed a twenty-six-yard pass to Ronnie Spurgeon. After two penalties were called on Dalton and two penalties were called on Cedartown, the 'Dogs had the ball on the fifteen-yard line. As the clock ticked down to zero, Cobb got off a thirty-two-yard field goal that split the uprights, giving Cedartown a thrilling 9–7 victory.

Putting together back-to-back wins against Gordon Central and Haralson County, the 'Dogs went on the road to play Villa Rica. After taking a 23–0 drubbing from Carrollton, Hill knew that Wildcat coach Frank Vohun would have his team ready for Cedartown.

Wildcat Tot Hudson returned a first-quarter punt eighty-two yards for the touchdown to give Villa Rica an early 7–0 lead. Unable to mount an offensive scoring threat, Cedartown got on the scoreboard when David Chandler intercepted a pass and returned the ball to the Villa Rica six-yard line. Odell Abram scored on his third carry, and Jeremy Cobb added the point after to tie the score at 7–7. With two minutes and thirty-three seconds remaining in the half, Hooper threw to Isaac Schofield for a sixty-yard scoring pass that was brought back to the Villa Rica forty-yard line because of a clipping penalty. On the next play, Spurgeon hauled in a pass from Hooper for the touchdown, and the Bulldogs led 14–7 at the half.

Early in the fourth quarter, taking advantage of a short Cedartown punt, Villa Rica quickly moved the ball to the seven-yard line. On third down from the three-yard line, Reggie Poole broke through the line and put a bruising hit on the Villa Rica ball carrier at the five-yard line. Villa Rica settled for the field goal, and Cedartown held a slim 14–10 lead. Starting at the twenty-yard line, the Bulldogs put together an eighty-yard scoring drive that used all but thirty-seven seconds of the quarter and secured the 21–10 win. Although Villa Rica scored 10 points, the Bulldog defense held the Wildcats to seventy-seven yards of total offense. The 'Dogs were so dominant at one point in the game that they had pushed the Wildcats back to their eight-yard line. Facing third down with thirty-seven yards to go to get a first down, Coach Vohun elected to punt on third down.

After a 34–0 shutout over Dade County, the Bulldogs set out on the road for the fifth time in six games to face AA perennial power Cartersville. The Purple Hurricanes were on a two-game slide with tough losses to Pepperell and Carrollton. Like every other good program in North Georgia, the Hurricanes would be ready to play when the No. 2 Bulldogs came to town.

The Cartersville game plan was to go to the air and force the Bulldogs to spread out their defense, which would allow more room for the Hurricanes to run inside. The Bulldog pass rush and solid defensive coverage skills in the secondary kept the 'Canes in check for most of the night.

Pushed back to the four-yard line and under a heavy Cedartown rush, Cartersville's punter had to hurry his kick. This resulted in a short punt that Brandon Lewis returned to the Hurricane twelve-yard line. Two plays later, Hooper carried the ball in for the score, putting the 'Dogs in front 7–0. Cartersville answered when Brad Maddox hit Victor Davis for a sixty-four-yard touchdown. The missed extra point made the score Cedartown 7, Cartersville 6. Cedartown's David Chandler returned the kickoff to the forty-nine-yard line. Odell Abrams ran for twenty-five yards, Hooper kept the ball for fourteen yards and Hoke ran it in from the one-yard line to extend the 'Dogs lead to 14–6.

Late in the first half, Hooper came under intense pressure from Cartersville's defensive front and threw a desperation pass that was intercepted by Davis and returned sixty yards for the score. The unsuccessful attempt for the 2-point conversion made the score Cedartown 14, Cartersville 12. With less than two minutes to play in the half, Cedartown fumbled the football, and Cartersville recovered it at the Cedartown thirty-nine-yard line. The Hurricanes had the ball with a first down inside the ten-yard line when Reggie Poole reached quarterback Maddox for a nine-yard loss. Trying to avoid being sacked again, Maddox threw an errant pass that was ruled to be intentional grounding. The penalty moved the ball back to the twenty-seven-yard line. From there, the forty-four-yard field goal sailed wide right, and the Bulldogs clung to a 2-point lead at the half.

The Bulldog defense dominated the second half, as Cartersville only made one serious scoring threat by faking a punt that took it inside Cedartown's twenty-yard line. The defense dug in, and on fourth down, Ken Veal sacked Maddox for an eleven-yard loss to seal the victory.

Rockmart opened the season with losses to three state powers: Gainesville, Villa Rica and Carrollton. It followed that with a three-game winning streak before the renewal of one of the fiercest rivalries in the state. In the earlier days, the saying in Cedartown and Rockmart was that if you lost the game you had better win the fight after the game. The bitterness is not as intense as it once was, but whether you were 10-0 or 0-10, the Polk County championship was something worth fighting for.

Rockmart's Adrian Cooper took the opening kickoff eighty-eight yards for a touchdown, and the Yellow Jackets stung the Bulldogs early, taking a 6–0 lead. The Bulldogs answered with a fifty-four-yard touchdown drive to even the score at 6–6. Late in the second quarter, Reggie Poole intercepted a pass to set up another Bulldog touchdown. Jeremy Cobb missed his second extra-point attempt, and Cedartown led 12–6.

With one minute and one second left in the third quarter, Rockmart recovered a Cedartown fumble at the thirty-yard line. Four plays later, Denzel Darden ran twenty-two yards for a Rockmart touchdown. Russ Hunt's extra point was good, and Rockmart sat on a 13–12 lead early in the fourth quarter. Cedartown put together a nine-play drive that carried the ball to the three-yard line. On second down, Hooper was hit at the goal line. The ball popped free and was recovered by Rockmart at the five-yard line. The defense held, and Cedartown got the ball with three minutes and eight seconds remaining in the game. Hooper kept the ball for a gain of eleven yards to the twenty-five-yard line, but an unsportsmanlike conduct penalty pushed the 'Dogs back to the thirty-eight-yard line. Two more penalties and one pass completion found the Bulldogs with a fourth down and thirty-eight yards to go with the ball on the forty-nine-yard line. Hooper dropped back to pass and was smothered by Yellow Jacket defenders to seal the 13–12 upset for Rockmart.

The general conception was that Cedartown went into the Rockmart game overconfident and was looking ahead to its next game against No. 3 Carrollton. The loss to Rockmart pushed Cedartown back to No. 8 in the polls.

Carrollton's quarterback, David Rooks, had a 62.5 completion percentage entering the Cedartown game. On a rainy night and a muddy field, the all-state quarterback was ineffective as he completed only seven passes out of twenty-eight attempts for 102 yards and one touchdown. Cedartown's defense buckled the Carrollton offensive line as Preston Sewell and Geoffrey Fraizer each had nine tackles and six quarterback sacks as the Trojans were held to negative rushing yardage. Cedartown had two first-half touchdowns and contained the Carrollton offense for the 14–7 victory and control of region 6AA.

After shaking off the pesky LaFayette Ramblers, the 'Dogs set their sights on Pepperell for the region championship. A loss to the Dragons would drop Cedartown to third place in the region and force it to go on the road in the playoffs.

Trailing by 4 points midway through the final period, Cedartown recovered a fumble at the seven-yard line and thwarted a Pepperell drive that would have sealed the win for Pepperell. With the clock winding down, Cedartown began to pick up momentum as it moved the ball over the midfield stripe. Managing just one yard on the first two plays, Hooper attempted to toss a pass over the Dragon defenders to Reggie Poole. Pepperell's Fred Collins got his hand on the ball and tried to deflect it away. Poole was able to get his hands on the ball, make the catch and run untouched into the end zone. Cobb's kick put the 'Dogs on top 17–14.

On the ensuing kickoff, Cobb's kick went out of bounds. Instead of taking possession of the ball at the thirty-five-yard line, Pepperell elected to receive another kickoff. On the next kick, Pepperell's Johnny Ray Wheat fielded the ball before it could roll out of bounds and streaked along the sidelines for a sixty-six-yard touchdown sprint. Pepperell spoiled the Bulldogs' hopes of another region championship as the 'Dogs were defeated 21–17.

Coach Hill's main concern going into the first round of the playoffs was whether the players would be able to regain the confidence and have the will to win after the disappointing loss to Pepperell. He was even more concerned when South Forsyth pushed the Bulldog defense down the field and scored a first-quarter touchdown to take a 7–0 lead.

The Bulldogs continued to struggle until late in the first half, when Brandon Lewis returned a Forsyth punt for a forty-yard touchdown. Moments later, Reggie Poole sacked quarterback Wesley Ellis, forcing a fumble that was recovered by LaJuan Hoke. Antowan Ammons gained sixteen yards on a reverse to set up Bradley Cook's two-yard touchdown burst. Jeremy Cobb's kick missed the mark, and Cedartown led 14–7.

The 'Dogs began the third quarter with a nine-play, seventy-four-yard scoring drive as James Hooper kept the ball on the option and scored. Cobb's kick was true, and the Bulldogs had a 20–7 lead. South Forsyth pulled to within a touchdown when Nathan Samples connected with Brian Brannon on a halfback pass. Cedartown received the kickoff and drove the ball fifty-nine yards in ten plays to run out the clock.

The Dacula Falcons were unranked at the beginning of the season. They cracked the top ten at week four and buried every opponent in their path. Coach Hill stated that if the Bulldogs didn't pick up the intensity, they might be headed for another game like the one the previous season against Josey.

After a scoreless first quarter, Dacula marched forty-two yards in thirteen plays to take a 6–0 lead. Cedartown fumbled the kickoff to set up the Falcons' next score. On the next kickoff, Cedartown once again turned the ball back over to Dacula, and the Falcons answered with 6 more points to build the lead to 18–0. Deep in a hole, the Bulldogs showed life when Ronnie Spurgeon caught a James Hooper pass and ran for a thirty-eight-yard touchdown. Cobb's kick for the extra point made the score Dacula 18, Cedartown 7. Dacula went to work with one minute and twenty-eight seconds left on the clock and drove down to score its fourth touchdown of the half and take a 24–7 lead at intermission.

Cedartown could not find any offensive momentum in the second half and continued to turn the ball over. The five Cedartown fumbles that were recovered by Dacula were more than enough to put an end to another terrific Cedartown season.

James Malone, Bo Perry, Ken Veal, Reggie Poole and Ronnie Spurgeon were all named to either the Associated Press or the *Atlanta Journal-Constitution* all-state team.

1997

Citing a lack of depth, Coach Hill prepared a team that was mixed with experienced, skilled personnel and untested underclassmen. James Hooper, Ronnie Spurgeon, Odell Abram and Isaac Schofield returned on the offensive side of the ball. Defensive journeymen Ken Veal, James Malone, David Chandler and Brandon Lewis also returned.

Hill must have been confident in his troops, but with the way the Bulldogs had faded at the end of the previous season, he had to wonder if there was anything that could provide the spark to get them past Villa Rica, Pepperell and Carrollton. Just because they made it to the second round of the playoffs didn't guarantee that they would even make the finals. After all, four teams from 6AA had advanced to the second round of the previous year's playoffs.

The Bulldogs would begin the season with the seemingly insurmountable task of trying to win a third straight game against Dalton. Bill Chappell had moved on to the rocking chair on the front porch, and no one knew how the players would react to a new coach.

James Hooper hit Ronnie Spurgeon for a six-yard touchdown strike in the first quarter. Odell Abram added a six-yard touchdown run in the fourth as the Bulldogs shut out the Catamounts 14–0. This was the first time in history that any team had beaten Dalton three times in a row.

After picking up easy wins over Gordon Central and Haralson County, the 'Dogs played host to Villa Rica. Cedartown scored first when Odell Abram went over from four yards out. Villa Rica responded by driving the ball seventy-eight yards to tie the game. The Wildcats scored again to open the second quarter, but the kick for the extra point sailed wide, and Villa Rica went up 13–7. Cedartown came right back as James Hooper hit Antowan Ammons for a thirty-four-yard pass completion and Ronnie Spurgeon for a fourteen-yard gain. Hooper carried the ball over from the two-yard line, and Hayes's kick put the 'Dogs back out front 14–13.

Cedartown scored another touchdown in the third quarter when Abram broke loose for a twenty-two-yard score and looked to have the game in hand when Hooper carried the ball into the end zone from the seven-yard line. With seven minutes and twenty-two seconds remaining in the game, Wildcat running back Craig Phillips sprinted through the Cedartown line to score. The 2-point conversion attempt was unsuccessful, and the Wildcats trailed 28–19.

Cedartown was unable to move the ball and punted to Villa Rica. The Wildcats moved the ball downfield and scored when quarterback Lamaze

Hindsman completed a sixteen-yard touchdown pass from Walt Cash. The point after kick made it a 2-point game at 28–26. The Bulldogs were pinned down with a fourth down and twenty yards to go. James Hooper scrambled to the twenty-five-yard line and fumbled the football. Ammons picked up the football and ran it out to the thirty-five-yard line to give Cedartown a first down and the win.

With four wins and no losses, Cedartown had moved up to sixth in the AA poll, but the Dade County Wolverines didn't show the Bulldogs much respect by taking a 24–12 lead early in the fourth quarter. Cedartown stormed back with two fourth-quarter touchdowns to seal the win.

The 'Dogs eased by Cartersville 26–14 but lost Hooper, who went out with a concussion and would miss the next game against Rockmart.

In a long-awaited rematch of the previous year's Polk County championship, sophomore Schyuler Pace stepped in for the injured James Hooper as the Bulldogs shut down the Rockmart offense and cruised to a 48–7 victory. Ronnie Spurgeon was the star of the game, pulling in four passes, but two of them were difficult catches that required some acrobatic maneuvers.

Carrollton was ranked No. 2 in the state and was just as anxious to repay Cedartown for the previous year's defeat as Cedartown had been to pay back Rockmart. Cedartown led Carrollton 13–7 at halftime, but Carrollton scored 15 unanswered points in the second half to give Carrollton the win and put the Trojans in control of region 6AA.

A win over LaFayette followed by a disappointing loss to Pepperell left Cedartown in fourth place in the region. With no fuel left in the tank, the once powerful Bulldog machine sputtered back up the road to Forsyth County, where it completely ran out of gas and ended a successful yet less than stellar 1997 season. After winning seven in a row to begin the season, Cedartown lost three out of the last four games.

Ken Veal, Ronnie Spurgeon and James Malone were named to the *Atlanta Journal-Constitution* or Associated Press all-state team. James Malone went on to play football for the University of Alabama at Birmingham. Ken Veal was a three-year letterman for the University of Georgia Bulldogs.

1998

As if region 6AA wasn't tough enough, now Central of Carrollton had dropped down from AAA to give the region five powerful football programs.

To make matters worse, Cedartown had lost all of its key players and was looking at a rebuilding season. Perhaps by now Coach Hill was beginning to believe that Cedartown quarterbacks grew on trees, but Schyuler Pace had limited game experience, and sitting next to him on the depth chart was the cocky little sophomore Joey King. King, who was the nephew of a former Bulldog, Joe Kines, had already informed everyone he knew that he was going to be the next great Cedartown quarterback. Joey had lovability about him that made everyone want to believe that he would indeed become the next great Cedartown quarterback.

Antowan Ammons returned at wide receiver and had the skills to play running back. Bradley Cook was expected to carry the brunt of the load at fullback. Coach Hill believed handing the ball to Cook behind offensive linemen Jamey Diamond and Adrian Huggins would be the most successful way to run the football, especially early in the season

Most of the experience on the defensive side of the football was in the secondary that returned starters David Chandler, Brandon Lewis and Josh James. Jamey Diamond and Adrian Huggins would also bolster the defensive line.

Dalton said that it wanted to take a break, so Coach Hill went to another old rival, Rome, to open the 1998 season. Everyone had always marveled at how powerful the team would be if West Rome and East Rome ever combined schools. Well, in 1992, they combined to create Rome High, and the most they had to show for it so far was 1997's quarterfinal appearance. But Hill knew that didn't mean that it was going to be an easy pushover. Rome proved that by taking the season opener from the 'Dogs 23–14.

The 'Dogs came back in week two to beat LaFayette 34–14 but lost a close one to Central of Carrollton 14–7. A fourth-quarter rally was cut short when the Lions recovered the Bulldogs' attempted onsides kick.

Things would only get worse the next week when the undefeated Villa Rica Wildcats came to town and exposed Cedartown's weaknesses and defeated them handily by a score of 37–13. Schyuler Pace was injured and left the game in the second quarter. Hill shook the quarterback tree, and out fell Joey King. King completed his first six passes and led the Bulldogs to their first score, but he was unable to put together another successful series until the fourth quarter.

Seizing the opportunity to put another skilled player on the field, Coach Hill converted Schyuler Pace to wide receiver and handed the starting quarterback job to Joey King. The team responded with a newfound energy and jumped to a 20–0 first-quarter lead against Carrollton. The 'Dogs, aided by a forty-one-yard run by Bradley Cook, took the opening kickoff and drove seventy-five yards for the score. After a defensive stop, Cedartown's Brandon Lewis outran the Carrollton secondary and scored on a sixty-one-yard run. On the next Carrollton punt, it was Lewis again who ran the ball back to the Carrollton twenty-six-yard line. Three plays later, Cook scored on a nine-yard run. In the second quarter, Carrollton scored on a sixty-seven-yard touchdown pass from Mike Johnson to Reggie Brown and a nineteen-yard run by Martez Beasley to close the gap to 20–14.

Cedartown threatened again in the third quarter as the Bulldogs drove to the Carrollton thirteen-yard line, but a Justin Hayes field goal attempt missed its mark. Early in the fourth quarter, Carrollton took a 21–20 lead when Johnson completed a fade pass to Blake Sabo for the score. On Cedartown's next possession, Carrollton's Raffie Hunt intercepted a Joey King pass and returned it for a touchdown. After an exchange in possessions, Carrollton took advantage of a short field to drive in for the score and surge to a 35–20 lead. Cedartown continued its offensive assault when Joey King threw a forty-seven-yard touchdown pass to Antowan Ammons. On Carrollton's next possession, Martez Beasley dashed any hopes of a Cedartown comeback as he scampered fifty-five yards for a Trojan score to secure the victory.

Displaying a balance between the run and the pass, Cedartown buried Chattooga, 48–7. Jamey Diamond set the tone for the game by sacking the Chattooga quarterback four times for losses of 31 yards. Schyuler Pace and Antowan Ammons showed their versatility as ball carriers and pass receivers, each accounting for over 100 yards of offense. Joey King continued to be impressive as he threw two touchdown passes for 191 yards.

The Pepperell Dragons entered Cedartown Memorial Stadium ranked No. 10 in AA. Led by all-state running back Sydney Ford, the Dragons possessed one of the strongest running attacks in the state. Coming off a strong effort against Carrollton and a big win at Chattooga, Coach Hill believed the 'Dogs could win the game. Pepperell dominated the game behind Ford and an offense that ran for over three hundred yards while stuffing Cedartown's offense to negative fourteen yards rushing. The 37–0 shutout eliminated the Bulldogs' chances for a playoff berth and, with two wins and five losses, left them in danger of having a losing season.

Behind solid defensive play and improving offense, the Bulldogs rallied to win the last three games of the season and finished with five wins and five losses.

Brandon Lewis and Jamey Diamond were named to the *Atlanta Journal-Constitution* and the Associated Press all-state teams.

CHAPTER 14

LIVING THE DREAM

1999

Cedartown began the 1999 season ranked No. 12 in Class AAA. After six straight wins, including blowouts over Carrollton and Villa Rica, the 'Dogs had climbed to No. 3. Over in Lindale, Georgia, the Pepperell Dragons had their sights set on the same prize as Cedartown. Zach Burkhalter returned a punt fifty yards to set up Pepperell's first score. In the third quarter, the Dragons staged a time-consuming drive to take a 13–0 lead. Cedartown's offense, which had been averaging 35 points a game, was shut out for the first time.

Schyuler Pace intercepted a Haralson County pass at the thirty-yard line to preserve a 13–7 win over the upset-minded Rebels.

The Bulldogs eased through the remaining schedule and took on Westminster School in the first round of the playoffs. Cedartown got on the board first when linebacker Jamey Diamond made a big hit on the Westminster running back and caused a fumble. Cedartown's Tim Jones picked up the ball and ran twenty-nine yards for the score. The extra point attempt was missed, and Cedartown led 6–0. Two plays later, Diamond caused another fumble, giving the 'Dogs the ball on the Wildcats' thirty-yard line. King connected with Pace for the score. Greg Talley ran the ball over for the 2-point conversion, and the 'Dogs were up 14–0. Westminster was unable to move the ball and had to punt. Cedartown drove eighty-four yards in eleven plays to score as King threw to Pace for the score. The missed extra point made it a 20–0 game. Westminster responded with a seventy-six-yard drive to get on the board right before halftime. The missed extra point made the score 20–6.

Cedartown returned a favor in the third quarter when Kendrick Sewell fumbled at the Westminster forty-four-yard line. Trying to exploit the Cedartown pass defense, Westminster began to throw the ball. Sewell redeemed his fumble when he stepped in front of a Wildcat receiver and picked off a pass that he returned for a fifty-seven-yard touchdown. The 2-point conversion gave the 'Dogs a comfortable 28–6 lead. Westminster fought back, driving sixty-five yards to score on a flea flicker pass thrown by the flanker, Matt Calamari. The 2-point try was good, and the Wildcats drew closer at 28–14. Lady Luck began to find favor with Westminster when an errant Joey King pass was intercepted, setting up another Wildcat score and drawing the game closer at 28–21

Trying to run out the clock, Cedartown moved the ball on the ground. On fourth down, King tossed an eleven-yard completion to Pace. On the next play, King connected again with Pace for the touchdown and a 35–21 lead. Westminster took the kickoff and marched sixty-four yards in one minute and twenty-two seconds and now trailed the Bulldogs 35–28. Cedartown was unable to move the football and punted the ball back to Westminster. On the first play, Kendrick Sewell intercepted a pass to seal the victory for Cedartown.

Cedartown would now host undefeated Mitchell-Baker High School in the state quarterfinals. All-state quarterback Dondrial Pinkins led Mitchell-Baker. Many people believed that Pinkins was the best quarterback in the state. He had passed for over one thousand yards and run for over one thousand yards. Stopping him was the key to a Cedartown victory.

In the first quarter, Cedartown drove the ball down field and was about to score, but Joey King lost the football as he was trying to reach it out over the plane of the goal line. The ball rolled through the end zone for a touchback, and the ball went to the Eagles. After the turnover, the 'Dogs offense became sluggish. A twelve-yard Cedartown punt gave Mitchell-Baker the ball on the Cedartown thirty-six-yard line. It looked like the Bulldogs were going to escape the turnover when the Eagles running back was thrown for a twenty-yard loss. On the next play, Pinkins connected with Roddy White for a twenty-five-yard gain and a first down. On the next play, Paul Jones ran up the middle for the score. Pinkins kicked the extra point to put the Eagles in front 7–0.

The Cedartown defense shut down the Eagles' running game and pressured Pinkins. In the third quarter, Cedartown began to move the football. King hit on five of six passes, including a twenty-nine-yard touchdown pass to Pace. The extra point was missed, and the 'Dogs still trailed 7–6. The Cedartown defense continued to control the line of scrimmage and the momentum of the game. Matt Robinson stripped the ball from the Eagles' ball carrier, and Michael Gibson recovered on the Cedartown forty-four-yard line. King passed twice to Shiron Colvin and once to Pace before he kept the ball and ran around the right end for the fourteen-yard score. King fell on the ball in the end zone and got the wind knocked out of him. Pace came in to try the 2-point attempt. Following blockers Jamey Diamond and Kendrick Sewell, Pace ran untouched into the end zone to give the 'Dogs a 14–7 lead. Nearing the end of the game, Mitchell-Baker had the ball on the Cedartown thirty-five-yard line. Pinkins, under heavy pressure, made three pass attempts that were all broken up by the Bulldogs defenders.

The Cedartown Bulldogs would now have a high school football player's dream come true and play in the state semifinals in the Georgia Dome against the Hart County Bulldogs. Cedartown took a quick 8–0 lead when Joey King threw a fifty-yard touchdown pass to Shiron Colvin and ran for the 2-point conversion. After the scoring pass, Cedartown's passing game became ineffective. King would complete only two more passes. Cedartown was able to move the ball on the ground in the first half, but Hart County stuffed the run in the second half. In a disappointing performance by the 'Dogs, Hart County came away the victors 28–8.

After recording two hundred tackles for the season, Jamey Diamond was named the *Atlanta Journal-Constitution*'s Defensive Player of the Year. Schyuler Pace and Joey King were named to the *Atlanta Journal-Constitution* or the Associated Press all-state team.

2000

The new millennium brought some new opponents to the Bulldogs' schedule. AAAA powerhouses Pebblebrook and Creekside were expected to give the top-ranked Bulldogs a true test early in the season. Falling to both teams by a combined five points was no indication of how 2000 would unfold. The 'Dogs went on a nine-game winning streak and would not be seriously challenged until the quarterfinals of the state playoffs. Not being able to

Coach Hill (left) with booster club president Keith Ledbetter. *Courtesy of John Hill.*

capitalize on opportunities and making too many turnovers cost the Bulldogs their chance to return to the Georgia Dome and win a state championship.

Josh Woolfork and Kyle Camp were named to the *Atlanta Journal-Constitution* all-state team. Joey King was also named to the *Atlanta Journal-Constitution* all-state team. He finished his career at Cedartown with twenty-six wins and eight losses as a starter. He completed 304 out of 606 passes for over 4,700 yards with 54 touchdown passes. He is Cedartown's all-time leading quarterback for yards gained and touchdown passes. He played football for Carson Neumann College and is now the offensive coordinator for the Carrollton Trojans. Will he ever heed the call that Bear Bryant spoke of when he left Texas A&M for Alabama? "When mamma calls you just have to come running."

John Hill heeded the call to the fishing banks of southeast Georgia. After more than twenty-five years of coaching, he decided to retire. His major goal for Cedartown football was to leave the program in better condition than it had been when he took over. As athletic director, he was instrumental in the development of Cedartown High athletic facilities, which blossomed into a top-notch venue for all sports. Going down the list of high school football coaches with the most wins, John Hill's name will always be near the top.

2001

Everett Kelley was chosen to replace Coach Hill. Everett had grown up in Cedartown and played quarterback under Jimmy Hightower. He returned to Cedartown under Hill's tenure and was very instrumental in the success of the team. He and Kenny Jolly were teachers at the middle school. They watched over the players as they developed and had a strong bond with them when they became high school players. Coach Hill left Everett with a team that had the potential to go all the way. All he had to do was let the system run the way it usually did, and great things could happen.

Kelley's first order of business was to find a quarterback to replace Joey King. He had been tutoring his son Jacob to play quarterback since midget league. Everett's longtime friend and classmate, Allen Hunt, had been bringing his son Sam along to one day play quarterback for Cedartown. Everett decided to play them both in a platoon system. His detractors believed that Cedartown couldn't win playing two quarterbacks.

Playing both quarterbacks, Cedartown rolled through teams like Pebblebrook, Carrollton, Pepperell and Stephens County. Its first test was supposed to be against all-state running back Michael Cooper and undefeated Screven County. Cooper returned the opening kickoff eighty yards for the touchdown, but the play was called back on a penalty. The Cedartown defense shut down Cooper just as it had shut down every running back on the schedule, from Pebblebrook's Brent Thomas to Pepperell's Breon Ford. Shiron Colvin returned an interception eighty-one yards for a score. Verdis Boone picked up a fumble and raced seventy-two yards for the touchdown. Jacob Kelley tossed a six-yard scoring strike to Kendrick Sewell. Sam Hunt threw a sixty-two-yard touchdown pass to DeMarcus James as Cedartown had little problems beating Screven County 38–20.

The Bulldogs had some unfinished business in the Georgia Dome. The team was well prepared and focused when it took the field against Fitzgerald. The Purple Hurricanes had tied Coffee County in the first game of the season, but no one had come close to beating them since.

Cedartown took the opening kickoff and drove to the Fitzgerald twenty-eight-yard line before turning the ball over on downs. Fitzgerald was driving toward an apparent score when Matt Robinson forced a fumble that Shiron Colvin recovered at the two-yard line. Cedartown drove ninety-eight yards and scored when Sam Hunt threw an eleven-yard touchdown pass to Drew Robinson. Fitzgerald answered with a fifty-four-yard drive for a touchdown and took a 9–7 lead just before the half when it added a field goal. With

Coach Everett Kelley with son Jacob and daughter-in-law Dana. *Courtesy of Everett Kelley.*

sixteen seconds to go in the half, Sam Hunt connected with Shiron Colvin as he streaked down the left sideline for a sixty-four-yard touchdown pass.

Cedartown opened the second half with a fifty-four-yard scoring drive to make the score 21–9. The Bulldogs stopped the Hurricanes at the one-yard line but fumbled on the next play to set up a Fitzgerald score. Cedartown drove seventy-four yards and scored when Hunt connected with Colvin on a twenty-one-yard touchdown pass. Fitzgerald put together a drive to the Cedartown twenty-one-yard line. Quarterback Tyler Pruitt mishandled the snap, and Matt Robinson picked up the ball and ran for a seventy-nine-yard touchdown to put the 'Dogs ahead to stay. Not to be outdone, Matt's twin brother, Drew, intercepted a pass and raced sixty-seven yards for the touchdown that sealed the victory and brought the state championship game to Cedartown.

When Shiron Colvin was told about LaGrange's history of playing in and winning state championships, he responded, "We know they've got some tradition, but we've got our own tradition."

INDEX

ABOUT THE AUTHOR

William Austin has deep-seated roots in Cedartown. Three of his great-grandfathers enlisted in the Confederate army in Cedartown and served the duration of the war. As a youth, William washed cars and learned auto mechanics working for Bill Byrom at Byrom's Auto Center on the corner of West Avenue and College Street. As a delivery boy for Hunt's Drug Store, he knew the location of every street in town and most of the residents. While serving a four-year enlistment in the U.S. Air Force, he followed the Bulldogs by subscribing to the *Cedartown Standard* in places as far away as Korea. It was upon returning to Cedartown and enrolling at Floyd Jr. College that the door to literature was opened. He was introduced to the classic stories and great storytellers like Shakespeare, Ibsen and Hemingway. Having no stories to write, he lucked into the world of horse racing. Sitting in the saddle astride the world's most dynamic athlete, he relished having a job that was more fun than work. In 1987, he married the former Jeanene Cook, daughter of Reverend and Mrs. J. Shelby Cook. Traveling the racehorse circuit was not an ideal way to raise their small son, Benjamin. In 1989, William and his family settled in Aiken, South Carolina, where he is a machine technician for Bridgestone/Firestone. Jeanene teaches high school, and Benjamin is the dean of students at Catawba College in North Carolina. Now, with a lifetime of experiences, there are stories to write, and this one is about one of William Austin's favorite subjects.